A FAMILY COOKBOOK FROM

Neiman Marcus

Published by Neiman Marcus InCircle®

Dallas, Texas

Published by Neiman Marcus InCircle, a division of The Neiman Marcus Group, Inc.

Printed by R.R. Donnelley & Sons Company.

Distributed in the United States and internationally by Harcourt Brace & Company, New York, San Diego and London.

Type set by The Word Worker, Seattle, WA.

Manufactured in the United States of America.

First Edition

10 9 8 7 6 5 4 3 2 1

ISBN 0-15-261697-7

Library of Congress Catalog Card Number: 93-084334

ACKNOWLEDGMENTS

Neiman Marcus InCircle would like to thank the following individuals for their time, effort and interest in *Pigtails and Froglegs:*

CONTRIBUTORS

To all InCirclers who submitted recipes demonstrating their interest in supporting children's causes. We regret the necessity to limit the number to 275 final choices.

Michael Jackson, whose commitment to the needs of all children is evident in the foreword which he wrote.

Stanley Marcus, Neiman Marcus' revered Chairman Emeritus and author of the preface to *Pigtails and Froglegs.*

CREATIVE GROUP

Chuck Jones, the distinguished InCircler whose witty illustrations set a fast pace for the entire book.

Clare Adams Kittle, who bore the responsibility for producing and coordinating all aspects of *Pigtails and Froglegs* from start to finish.

Laura Rivers, our senior editor and wordsmith of all text other than contributors'.

Matt O'Brien, who catalogued and typed all recipes.

Jan Edwards, whose skills in publicity have ensured a successful launch for *Pigtails and Froglegs.*

THE FOOD TEAM

Bob Jones, Neiman Marcus Vice President and Director of Food Service, who coordinated all testing and selection of recipes.

Alfons Konrad, Vice President, Food and Beverage, and the chefs at Four Seasons Hotels and Resorts in Washington, Chicago and Beverly Hills who lent their expertise to the testing of the recipes.

Jane Cabaniss Jarrell, who served as food editor and assisted with the recipes' testing phase.

NEIMAN MARCUS

Debby Posin of The Neiman Marcus Group, Inc., who provided advice throughout the entire project.

The InCircle staff whose input of ideas and energetic support made it possible to produce this book.

SPECIAL FRIEND

Duffy Keys, Vice President, Field Marketing of Four Seasons Hotels and Resorts, who enthusiastically joined in support of *Pigtails and Froglegs* from its inception.

Dedicated to everyone
who was a kid . . .
who is a kid . . .
who will always be a kid.

FOREWORD

Nourish This Child

To a child, food is something special. It isn't just a delicious taste or the vitamins that build a healthy body. Food is love and caring, security and hope—all the things that a good family can provide. Remember when you were little and your mother made a pie for you? When she cut a slice and put it on your plate, she was giving you a bit of herself, in the form of her love. She made you feel safe and wanted. She made your hunger go away, and when you were full and satisfied, everything seemed all right. Because that satisfied feeling was in the pie, you were nourished from a deep level. Food is something we all need physically, but so is the love, the deeper nourishment, that turns us into who we are.

Think about how necessary it is to nourish a child with a bit of yourself when you use this book. It is full of delicious things. Every recipe has an extra ingredient of caring, because the people who wrote them were thinking of the children. They were especially thinking of those who aren't able to take nourishment for granted because they are poor, sick or disabled. These are the children who need food to heal. The theme of "Heal the World," which has been close to my heart, is the central theme of this book, also. Here are recipes for the spirit. Please make them with that in mind. Your child is a growing spirit that can be knit strong with love. When you break an egg and measure a cup of flour, you are magically mixing the gift of life. The food's proteins and minerals will turn into bones and muscles, but your feeling as you cook will turn directly into a soul.

It makes me happy to think that the needs of children's spirits are at last becoming important in this world. Children have no power to end wars directly or to mend age-old differences. All they can do is be themselves, to shine with gratitude and joy when love is turned their way. Yet isn't that ultimately the greatest power? In the eyes of a child you become the source of joy, which lifts you into the special category of caregiver and life-provider. You may think that your apple pie has only sugar and spice in it. A child is wiser—with the first bite, he knows that this special dish is the essence of your love. Enjoy!

Michael Jackson
Heal the World Foundation

CHUCK JONES'
8/15/93-

LEGENDARY ILLUSTRATOR AND ANIMATOR

Chuck Jones

Several years ago we organized an InCircle outing to the world-famous San Diego Zoo® and Wild Animal Park. We were delighted to discover that one of the InCirclers who signed up was legendary animator-director, Chuck Jones. Delighted and fascinated by the wondrous experience at the park, many of us were equally delighted as we watched Chuck deftly take "notes" in his sketchbook throughout the tour. The experience stuck with us. So, when we decided to produce a second InCircle cookbook, we thought immediately of those delightful zoological "notes" and invited Chuck to illustrate the book in his special style. We are so glad he agreed; we know you will be, too.

In a career spanning more than sixty years, Chuck Jones has made more than 250 films, won three Academy Awards, and been nominated for six others. He has created internationally acclaimed characters including Pepé Le Pew, Road Runner and Wile E. Coyote as well as being one of the three or four "fathers" of Bugs Bunny, Daffy Duck, Porky Pig and twenty to thirty more Warner Bros. characters. His accomplishments are far too numerous to list, but included are the perennial favorite television specials; Dr. Seuss' *How the Grinch Stole Christmas, Horton Hears a Who,* and six other half-hour specials which have become classics in their own right.

We feel extremely fortunate to have two new cover characters, and special illustrations throughout our cookbook, created expressly for us by our favorite master of animation, Chuck Jones.

PREFACE

Pigtails and Froglegs should be a worthy successor to *Pure & Simple,* for both have their genesis in the recipes from Neiman Marcus InCircle® customers. *Pure & Simple* contributors continue to be rewarded by having their proportionate share of the authors' royalties donated to the charities of their choice. These same institutions were enriched by a total of $250,000, through spring 1993, as a result.

Pigtails and Froglegs' authors' royalties will be divided between four outstanding national organizations, which are devoted, naturally, to the care and welfare of children. Through this method of distribution, each of the groups should receive a lump sum, large enough to help develop or execute a program benefitting a significant number of kids—programs as varied as the recipes in *Pigtails and Froglegs* and as geographically different as Corpus Christi, Texas is from Camden, Maine.

This is as it should be, for children come in countless varieties, as do their food tastes and preferences.

When I was growing up in the first two decades of the century, children ate what was served them—not what they had seen on the TV programs—because we didn't have television at the time, and there wasn't too much tolerance for the gastronomic idiosyncrasies of five- or ten-year-olds.

The hamburger hadn't been invented then, nor were pizzas and hot dogs available at the corner drug stores. Vitamins had not been discovered, but cod liver oil, a horrible-tasting derivative of a noble fish, was forced down youngsters' throats. Phillips' Milk of Magnesia®, castor oil and, finally, Calomel were prescribed to counteract the varying degrees of overeating and upset stomachs.

Not only has food preparation for children improved, but so have medications. Both have become more varied and palatable. Kids don't rely on Mom's advice for either one, for TV has become the overwhelming influence in the lives of young and old alike.

If you concur with this appraisal, then it makes sense for all parents and other readers of this book to encourage the producers, broadcasters, and licensees of their air channels to help feed the minds of our children with nutritious entertainment and education, instead of the constant diet of violence and gunfire.

Only then can we have children whose minds are as well-fed as their bodies.

Stanley Marcus
Chairman Emeritus, Neiman Marcus

TABLE OF CONTENTS

OUR CHARITIES

Dear Readers,

Selecting the charities to benefit from royalties on our second recipe book, *Pigtails and Froglegs*, was not an easy task. First, we polled several Neiman Marcus executives and InCircle members regarding the possible candidates (over two hundred and all richly deserving). After several months we narrowed the field to four finalists which represent a broad range of services to children. While *Pigtails and Froglegs* was conceived as a light-hearted approach to family cooking, its more serious side was never out of our thinking process. On behalf of all members of InCircle, that select group of Neiman Marcus customers, we sincerely hope that it has met its goal to help bring medical care, nurturing and ombudsman services to children everywhere.

Billy J. Payton
Vice President, Marketing and Customer Programs
Neiman Marcus

Childhelp USA

Founded in 1959 by Sara O'Meara and Yvonne Fedderson, Childhelp USA cares for hurt, abused and neglected children and is today the largest national nonprofit charity combating child abuse. The California-based organization offers the only national crisis line for child abuse, 1-800-4-A-CHILD. This hot line handles more than 360 thousand calls each year from across the United States and is open 24 hours a day, every day of the year.

The Village of Childhelp West in Beaumont, California has cared for severely abused and neglected children ages two through twelve for more than thirteen years. A staff of 150, including therapists, teachers, social workers, nurses and physicians, assist the children around the clock. An East Coast Village has recently opened in Culpeper County, Virginia.

Childhelp also conducts educational programs, public service announcements and research projects covering a wide range of child abuse prevention topics.

Pediatric AIDS Foundation

This is the only nonprofit organization created specifically to confront medical problems unique to children infected with HIV/AIDS. PAF is focused specifically on creating a future that will offer hope to these children and their families. These goals include educating communities with a national Parent Education Program and finding effective therapies and ways to block transmission from a mother to her newborn. PAF's co-founder, Elizabeth Glaser, whose presence at the 1992 Democratic National Convention so moved people, is justifiably proud of the fact that the Foundation's administrative overhead is held to 5 percent, greatly attributable to the efforts of countless volunteers. Given the unsettling fact that there are currently 20 thousand American children infected with HIV, the Pediatric AIDS Foundation has its work cut out for it.

St. Jude Children's Research Hospital

What most people know about St. Jude is that it was founded in 1962 by the late entertainer Danny Thomas, who was facing a crisis in his life. What is less known is that while about 150 children are treated daily in the Memphis facility, less than 50 of these are confined to the hospital. Children are referred by physicians all over the country for the catastrophic childhood diseases such as cancer, juvenile diabetes and now, AIDS. No child has ever been turned away for reason of race, religion, creed or ability to pay. Of all of St. Jude's accomplishments, the Hospital is most proud to have brought the survival rate for childhood cancer from less than 5 percent to 60 percent overall.

Special Olympics International

Founded in 1968 by the Joseph P. Kennedy Jr. Foundation for the benefit of citizens with mental retardation, Special Olympics has grown to global status under the dedicated guidance of Eunice Kennedy Shriver and her husband, Sargent Shriver. Through Special Olympics, persons with mental retardation train and compete in a variety of sports which, in turn, help to develop physical coordination, fitness, self-esteem and friendship. A vital aspect of Special Olympics' success is the active participation of more than 500 thousand community volunteers serving as coaches, drivers, game officials and in other capacities. Thanks to their efforts, millions of children and adults with mental retardation have participated in Special Olympics in more than one hundred countries.

THE FOOD TEAM

During the launch of our first cookbook, *Pure & Simple,* our friends at Four Seasons Hotels and Resorts approached us with an enthusiastic request to be involved in our next cooking/publishing venture. Knowing Four Seasons to be outstanding partners as our official InCircle hotel group, we were more than happy to oblige. Alfons Konrad, who is Vice President of Food and Beverage for Four Seasons, charged his top executive chefs with the responsibility of testing the hundreds of recipes in our family cookbook. (But only after our Food Service Vice President and Director, Bob Jones, made the initial selection of those recipes to be tested by Konrad's team.) So, now the result is dishes that are not only kid-approved, by testament of the mothers and others who submitted them, but dishes that may well turn up on Four Seasons menus across the country.

R. Wray (Bob) Jones

Vice President and Director of Food Service, Neiman Marcus

Bob Jones (no relation to Chuck) has been a creative force in food services for more than forty years, twenty of them overseeing Neiman Marcus restaurants coast to coast. Under his direction, the store's The Zodiac® restaurant in Dallas has won the Restaurant Hall of Fame award, plus many kudos from customers for the menus during the store's famous Fortnight® promotions. Jones is a frequent speaker at universities and national meetings, and often a judge in restaurant design competitions. In 1990 he received the coveted Silver Plate Award from the International Food Manufacturers. Over the years he has authored numerous cookbooks and been involved in the development of others such as Neiman Marcus' popular *Pure & Simple*, and now, *Pigtails and Froglegs.*

Our Chefs from the Four Seasons Hotels and Resorts

Rene Bajeux
Executive Chef, Four Seasons Hotel at Beverly Hills

A native of Alsace-Lorraine, Chef Bajeux spent twenty years at restaurants in Paris, Montreal and Chicago before joining Four Seasons' Resort when it opened in 1990 at Wailea, Maui. To the islands he brought a melting pot of international experience, and from the islands he discovered and rediscovered many cooking techniques, ingredients and seasonings. Now, he has brought his global philosophy and skills to Gardens restaurant at Four Seasons Hotel at Beverly Hills.

Mark Baker
Executive Chef, Four Seasons Hotel Chicago

Although this Boston native's first culinary experiments were right out of Julia Childs' original rich repertoire, he now emphasizes healthful cooking employing fresh, regional products and great imagination in contemporary American cuisine. He is the recipient of many honors in the food world and a veteran of fine kitchens from Four Seasons Boston to the elysian fields of the famous Greenbriar Hotel.

William Douglas McNeill
Executive Chef, Four Seasons Hotel Washington, D.C.

A graduate of the Great Western Hotel School of Oban, Scotland, Chef McNeill apprenticed at the famous Gleneagles Hotel. He subsequently worked at five-star restaurants in Scotland, England and Switzerland before joining Four Seasons Hotels in Canada. Rigid rules have no place in his kitchen. Instead, fresh foods and boundless creativity are the ingredients that have Washingtonians and others singing the praises of his menus for the hotel's dining facilities, from the elegant Aux Beaux Champs to banquets to room service.

CHAPTER ONE

COLD PIZZA FOR BREAKFAST?

Not when there are so many other good things. And, they don't all follow the everybody-sits-down-together tradition. Our tastes have obviously matured into more international ones, if Toad-in-the-Hole and Huevos Rancheros are any indication. A sack of mini muffins could guarantee a prime seat on the school bus or control of the meeting agenda. And, imagine the surprise when one Sunday morning the whole family remembers that waffles and pancakes do not necessarily pop out of the freezer and into the toaster. But, just to be on the safe side, we've included a recipe for Breakfast Sausage Pizzas.

CHEESE-EGG SOUFFLÉ

Sandra Krusoff
Sherman Oaks, CA

This has become a favorite request of my kids when I do a brunch. It is easy to prepare and presents itself to be more difficult than it is. I make it the day before and bake it the day of the brunch.

2 tablespoons butter
25 to 30 thin slices egg bread, crusts removed
20 slices sharp Cheddar cheese
12 eggs, beaten
4 cups milk
Seasoned salt to taste

Generously butter a 9x13-inch baking dish. Place a layer of bread on bottom of pan and cover with half of the cheese slices. Repeat layering process. Beat eggs, milk and salt until well blended. Pour over bread and cheese. Cover tightly. Refrigerate overnight. Bring soufflé from refrigerator to room temperature. Preheat oven to 350°. Bake 45 minutes or until top is brown and puffy. **Serves 10 to 12.**

Serve soufflé with crisp bacon and coffee.

GRANNY'S OMELET

Lailee Bakhtiar, M.D.
Los Angeles, CA

This is an easy recipe for my toddler grandchildren; they can afford cholesterol in their diet for brain power!

16 ounces Cheddar cheese, shredded
1¼ cups croutons
2 cups milk
4 eggs, beaten
Dash of onion powder
4 ounces Cheddar cheese, grated

Put 16 ounces shredded cheese in bottom of 8-inch glass baking dish. Spread croutons on cheese. Beat together milk, eggs and onion powder and pour over the cheese-crouton mixture. Add remaining cheese to the top. Bake at 350° for 1 hour, or until firm. Slice like a pie. **Serves 2.**

Serve omelet with fresh fruit.

GUACAMOLE-STUFFED OMELET SUPREME

Brenda Goldberg
Houston, TX

I devised this California-style recipe when I wanted to put the avocados growing in my backyard to use. The perfect breakfast for four. Our kids say, *"We thought only money grew on trees!"*

2 large avocados, mashed
1 ripe tomato, finely chopped
½ small yellow onion, chopped
1 lemon, juiced
Salt and pepper to taste
1 tablespoon vegetable oil
4 eggs, beaten until foamy
4 large navel oranges, sliced
2 tablespoons sour cream

Combine avocados, tomato, onion, lemon juice and seasonings. Set aside. Heat oil in a large frying pan and pour in beaten eggs. When edges begin to brown, carefully turn omelet over. Cook another 2 minutes, then spoon guacamole mixture onto one end of the omelet. Carefully roll omelet to one side of pan until guacamole is completely enclosed. Adjust pan and turn heat to low, cover, and cook gently for another minute. Place omelet on a large platter and surround with sliced oranges. Top with sour cream and serve.
Serves 4.

Serve omelet with fried potatoes and English muffins.

HUEVOS RANCHEROS, KID-STYLE

Marilyn Hausman
Newport Beach, CA

This was a favorite recipe the whole family developed a taste for after our numerous cruises down the Mexican coast on our boat.

1 pound Cheddar cheese, grated
2 cans (4 ounces each) diced green chilies, drained, liquid reserved
12 eggs, beaten
Salt to taste
Pepper, freshly ground, to taste
8 corn tortillas
Salsa

Preheat oven to 350°. Butter 9x13-inch glass baking dish. Spread cheese over bottom of prepared dish. Sprinkle with chilies. Blend liquid reserved from chilies into eggs. Season with salt and pepper. Pour over cheese and chilies. Bake at 350° until eggs are set, about 40 minutes. Cut into squares. Serve with corn tortillas and salsa. **Serves 6.**

Serve Huevos Rancheros with orange juice.

GREEN EGGS AND HAM

Cindi & Robert D. Colvin
Houston, TX

This recipe was inspired by Dr. Seuss' *"Green Eggs and Ham."* Our kids wanted to try *"Green Eggs"* so we added an avocado.

4 eggs
4 tablespoons water
2 ripe avocados, mashed
2 slices precooked ham

Scramble eggs, water and avocado on high heat. Must be done quickly or avocado will brown. Heat ham slices in skillet and top with egg mixture. **Serves 2.**

Serve with biscuits. Adults can add picante sauce for color.

LAGUNA MORNING EGGS

Debra Marcus
Laguna Niguel, CA

This is a favorite egg dish my husband discovered at a restaurant in San Diego. He loved it, so I was determined to duplicate it. Our three daughters enjoy it also.

2 packages (10 ounces each) frozen creamed spinach
2 eggs, separated, yolks only
3 tablespoons lemon juice, freshly squeezed
½ cup butter, divided
12 medium eggs
6 English muffins, split
2 cans artichoke bottoms, total of 12 bottoms
2 tablespoons dill

Microwave creamed spinach for 7 to 10 minutes, following package instructions.

For the hollandaise sauce, blend 2 slightly beaten egg yolks and lemon juice with a wooden spoon. Add ¼ cup butter. Heat over very low heat, stirring constantly until butter is melted. Add remaining ¼ cup butter, stirring until butter is melted and sauce thickens. The secret to an excellent hollandaise sauce is to cook slowly to prevent curdling. Set aside to serve over eggs. Poach 12 eggs. Split the English muffins. Then place under the broiler until toasted.

Arrange your Laguna Morning Eggs as follows: Place an artichoke bottom on each toasted muffin half. Spoon creamed spinach over the artichoke bottom and muffin. Place one poached egg on each muffin. Finally, spoon your hollandaise sauce over each completed muffin and sprinkle with dill. **Makes 12.**

Garnish each plate with fresh seasonal fruit and serve.

MEXICAN-STYLE SCRAMBLED EGGS

Leslie Marie Price
Pasadena, TX

This is a recipe my friend Maggie prepared for her family on Sundays at breakfast.

Tortillas:

2½ cups flour
½ cup shortening
¾ teaspoon salt
½ to 1 cup water, heated

Mexican-Style Eggs:

½ onion, diced
1 jalapeño pepper, finely diced
2 teaspoons butter
4 eggs, beaten

Tortillas: Cut shortening into flour and salt, as if making pie crust. Add very hot water, enough to make ingredients form dough. After dough is made, divide into good-sized knots and roll out flat. Cook over medium heat on griddle, for 2 minutes on each side or until lightly browned.

Mexican-Style Eggs: Sauté onions and jalapeño in butter. Beat eggs and stir into onions and peppers. Stir until cooked. Fill freshly made tortillas with egg mixture and serve. **Serves 2.**

TRIPLE CHEESE OMELET

Anna Imm
Katy, TX

I've been married twenty years, but I only made up this recipe last year. It's our favorite brunch.

2 tablespoons oil
2 tablespoons onion, chopped
2 tablespoons red pepper, chopped
2 tablespoons green bell pepper, chopped
3 eggs
1 slice American cheese
1 slice baby Swiss cheese
1 slice Monterey Jack cheese
1 slice ham, thinly sliced
¼ cup picante sauce

Add oil, onion and peppers to skillet and sauté gently until tender. Beat eggs in a bowl. Pour into skillet. Cook 2 minutes. Gently flip omelet and add cheeses and ham. Fold omelet and cook thoroughly. Remove from pan and top with picante sauce. **Serves 2.**

SPINACH-CHEESE OMELET

Gail Silverman
Dallas, TX

My mother always used milk in this recipe, but my sons like a firmer omelet. So, I've substituted cottage cheese for milk. I must say it stays on their forks better.

1 dozen eggs
1 container (24 ounces) cottage cheese
Salt to taste
2 packages (10 ounces each) chopped frozen spinach, thawed and drained
1 cup seasoned bread crumbs
5 tablespoons Parmesan cheese, grated

Combine all ingredients. Coat large frying pan with nonstick cooking spray. Pour into pan and cook covered over low heat for 30 minutes. Divide recipe in half for smaller frying pan.

To bake in oven pour into a glass-covered casserole dish coated with butter. Bake at 325° for 45 minutes or until metal prong comes out clean. **Serves 6.**

Note: Broccoli can be substituted for spinach.

Serve omelet with fresh fruit and muffins.

BREAKFAST SAUSAGE PIZZAS

Lynda Beal
Midland, TX

The friend who gave me this recipe has kids who are active in Boy Scouts. She freezes them for their camping trips.

2 sticks butter, softened
4 jars (5 ounces each) OLD ENGLISH® sharp cheese spread
2 pounds sausage
48 English muffins, halved

Combine butter and cheese spread. Blend well. Brown and drain sausage. Add to cheese mixture. Spoon mixture on top of muffins. Bake in 350° oven for 10 to 15 minutes. Pizzas can be frozen on cookie sheets, then placed in plastic bags to use when desired. Allow extra heating time for frozen pizza. Can be reheated in microwave. **Makes 48.**

RANCH BREAKFAST

Dorothy (Ajar) Apple
N. Hollywood, CA

My mother was a great cook and this was one of her best recipes. I serve it for brunch along with a couple of her other recipes I'm not prepared to share.

6 slices bacon, diced
3 cups potatoes, cooked and sliced
⅓ cup bell pepper, sliced
6 eggs
¼ teaspoon salt
1 cup Cheddar cheese, grated
1 can (7 ounces) green chili salsa

Cook bacon until crisp. Remove and drain off all but 3 tablespoons of fat. Add potatoes and bell peppers to drippings. Sauté until lightly browned. Break eggs over potatoes and sprinkle with salt. Add cheese and bacon, pour green chili salsa over, cover and cook at 350° for 25 to 30 minutes. **Serves 4 to 6.**

Serve Ranch Breakfast with bran muffins and Grandma's Apple Butter on page 173.

CHEESERS

Esther Feder
Suffern, NY

I invented this recipe twenty years ago when I first joined WEIGHT WATCHERS.® It was my substitute for blintzes, which I loved.

"We call it Cheesers!"

8 slices white bread
1 carton (8 ounces) cottage cheese
Sugar and cinnamon to taste
2 eggs, beaten
2 tablespoons butter or margarine

Flatten bread slices with a rolling pin or a large drinking glass. Mix cheese with sugar and cinnamon. Spread mixture on 4 slices of bread and cover with other 4 slices. Cut each sandwich into 4 pieces. Beat eggs. Dip sandwiches in egg and fry in butter or margarine until brown. **Makes 32.**

Note: Any kind of bread can be used.

Serve with large glass of orange juice.

TOAD-IN-THE-HOLE

Joan L. Sheppard
Godfrey, IL

Rachel (age 6) asked, *"How many princes will turn into frogs with this concoction?"*

1 slice of bread
2 teaspoons butter
1 egg
Salt to taste
Pepper to taste

Heat skillet. Butter 1 slice of favorite bread on both sides. Use the rim of a small juice glass to cut a hole in the middle of the bread. Put bread and "hole" in the skillet. Break 1 egg and put it in the hole, add salt and pepper. Turn bread when egg turns white, turn "hole" too. Serve with "hole" as lid to cover "toad." **Serves 1.**

Serve with a large glass of grape juice.

TRIPLE-T TOAST

Teresa Thrash
Tyler, TX

I remember my mother making applesauce toast but she doesn't recall it, so I've named mine Triple-T Toast for the three Thrash men in our family.

2 teaspoons butter
4 slices raisin bread or your favorite bread for toasting
1 teaspoon cinnamon
¼ cup sugar
½ cup applesauce
½ cup miniature marshmallows

Butter bread slices. Combine cinnamon and sugar; sprinkle heavily on bread. Toast bread in oven. After toasting, cover toasted bread with room temperature applesauce, more cinnamon-sugar and miniature marshmallows. Return toast to oven until marshmallows brown. **Serves 4.**

Serve with a tall glass of cold milk.

FLUFFS

Suzanne S. Brent
Amarillo, TX

A Saturday morning treat for my children—
they love these airy pancakes!

½ cup flour
¼ cup sugar
1 cup milk
1 tablespoon butter, melted
3 egg yolks
3 egg whites

Mix flour and sugar in bowl. Beat milk, melted butter and egg yolks until smooth, then blend with flour mixture. In a separate bowl, beat egg whites until stiff. Gently fold in egg whites. Pour small pancakes onto lightly oiled griddle. Cook until bubbles form on top and bottom begins to brown. Turn pancakes and continue cooking until lightly browned. **Serves 6.**

Serve with hot maple syrup and sausage patties.

FLUFFY PANCAKES

Virginia R. Bertrand
Kingwood, TX

These are a favorite on Saturday mornings when we have lots of time to be lazy. We also dye the batter green on St. Patrick's Day and make these in the shape of shamrocks. It guarantees good luck for the rest of the year.

"These pancakes are wonderful with melted butter and jam or syrup. They are always moist inside and the flavor never changes (even when Mom dyes them green)!"
Aimee Bertrand (age 10).

1 egg
¾ cup plus 2 tablespoons milk
2 tablespoons salad oil
1 cup flour
½ teaspoon salt
2 tablespoons baking powder
2 tablespoons sugar

Combine all ingredients and beat with mixer until smooth. Bake on an ungreased pancake griddle. They're best when made small using about ¼ cup batter. **Makes 12 small pancakes.**

Serve pancakes with fresh fruit and powdered sugar.

WAFFLES

Mrs. Arthur D. Cohen
Milton, MA

This is a light and delicious recipe for breakfast, but may be used for any time of the day.

1¾ cups flour
2 teaspoons baking powder
3 teaspoons sugar
½ teaspoon salt
3 egg yolks, beaten
1½ cups milk
⅓ cup vegetable oil
3 egg whites, beaten until stiff

Combine dry ingredients in mixing bowl. Combine egg yolks and milk. Stir into dry ingredients. Add cooking oil. Carefully fold in stiffly beaten egg whites. Do not overmix. Pour approximately ½ cup of batter onto a preheated griddle. Close and bake. **Serves 2.**

Variations:
Blueberry Waffles: ½ cup fresh or frozen blueberries, thawed and drained and folded into the batter.

Banana Crunch Waffles: Mix ⅓ cup mashed banana into the batter.

For the topping: Mix 1 small banana, sliced; ⅓ cup granola, and ¼ teaspoon nutmeg, if desired.

FUNNEL CAKES

Marilyn Kohn
E. Brunswick, NJ

My family enjoyed this in Amish country in Pennsylvania. I obtained the recipe and my children enjoyed making designs with the batter. CHILDREN NEED TO BE SUPERVISED.

2 eggs, beaten
1¼ cups milk
2 cups flour, sifted
1 teaspoon baking powder
½ teaspoon salt
2 cups oil

Combine eggs and milk. Add flour, baking powder and salt. Beat until smooth.

Heat oil in a deep skillet to 350°. Put batter in a funnel, plugging bottom with finger. Hold funnel over skillet, release finger, allowing batter to drop into oil in a swirl pattern, or make your own design. Fry until lightly browned, then turn and fry an additional 3 minutes.
Makes 4 cakes.

Dip Funnel Cakes in powdered sugar and serve with hot chocolate.

HOT CHOCOLATE MIX

Constance B. Norris
Oak Ridge, TX

This recipe is great for young children to make their own hot cocoa every morning. They say: *"Perfect every time."*

1 box (8 quarts) instant nonfat dry milk
1 container (16 ounces) NESTLÉ® QUIK®
6 ounces nondairy creamer
1½ cups powdered sugar

Mix all ingredients together and store in airtight container. Take ½ cup of mix and place in a mug. Add 1 cup of hot water and stir.
Makes 9 quarts.

Serve chocolate with tiny marshmallows.

BRAN MUFFINS

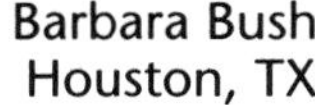

Barbara Bush
Houston, TX

When we opened the envelope postmarked "Houston, TX," we didn't quite know what to expect. Would it be barbecue? Pork rinds? Maine Lobster? To our surprise, it was for a very different, very tasty brand of bran muffin. Everyone at the InCircle office tried the recipe at home and declared them the best.

1 cup skim milk
2½ cups KELLOGG'S® ALL BRAN® cereal
¾ cup raisins
½ cup canola oil
5 large eggs, beaten, or egg substitute
1 cup honey
2 teaspoons vanilla
2½ cups whole wheat flour
1¼ teaspoons salt
2 tablespoons sugar
1 tablespoon baking powder
2 cups carrots, grated
2 apples, peeled and coarsely chopped
1 cup crushed pineapple, drained
¾ cup dates, chopped
12 prunes, cut into small pieces
1 cup pecans, chopped

Preheat oven to 350°. Combine milk, bran and raisins and let soak for 15 minutes, to soften. Add oil, eggs, honey and vanilla to the bran mixture. Mix together flour, sugar, baking powder, carrots, apples, pineapple, dates, prunes and nuts. Add to the bran mixture. Do not overmix. Fill greased muffin cups or muffin papers to top and bake for 30 minutes. Don't worry if you do not have all the dried fruits or nuts, just use what you have. **Makes 2 dozen.**

Serve with warm honey.

PUMPKIN-APPLESAUCE MUFFINS

Susan U. Briscoe
Dallas, TX

A good way to get some beta carotene into your children's diet. Great snack food, also.

1½ cups flour
1 cup whole wheat flour
1 cup sugar
1 tablespoon pumpkin pie spice
1 teaspoon baking soda
½ teaspoon salt (optional)
2 eggs, beaten or ½ cup egg substitute
1 can (16 ounces) solid-pack pumpkin
⅓ cup vegetable oil
1¼ cups chunky applesauce

In large bowl, combine flours, sugar, pumpkin pie spice, soda and salt. In medium bowl, combine beaten eggs, pumpkin and oil. Add pumpkin mixture to flour mixture and stir well. Add applesauce and mix until smooth. Don't overmix. Fill greased muffin cups. Bake in preheated 350° oven for 30 to 35 minutes. **Makes 16 muffins.**

BLUEBERRY MUFFINS

Mr. & Mrs. V. W. Sanders
Port Hueneme, CA

I learned to make this recipe in a home economics class at the age of twelve and after all these years it is still a family favorite. Easy to make for any age group and always a pleasure for adults and children alike.

1¼ cups flour
1 teaspoon soda
2 teaspoons cream of tartar
¼ cup plus 1 tablespoon sugar
½ teaspoon salt
1 egg
½ cup milk
⅓ cup shortening, melted
1 cup blueberries, drained

Sift together flour, soda, cream of tartar, sugar and salt. Make a well in the middle of the dry ingredients and add beaten egg, milk and melted shortening. Mix to combine. Lightly fold in blueberries. Bake in muffin tin at 400° for 18 to 20 minutes. **Makes 1 dozen.**

Serve muffins with Spinach-Cheese Omelet on page 23.

ORANGE BRAN MUFFINS

Karen Benning
Dallas, TX

I experimented with a lot of other recipes, but this one is the only one my kids will eat. Sometimes I substitute banana or blueberries for the orange, but they like this best of all.

My toddler daughter calls it *"nini,"* her word for candy.

2 cups KELLOGGS® ALL BRAN® cereal
1⅓ cups orange juice
1½ cups flour
1 teaspoon baking powder
⅔ cup sugar
2 tablespoons cinnamon
2 eggs, beaten
½ cup oil
3 tablespoons orange marmalade
1 teaspoon orange peel, grated

Mix cereal and orange juice together and set aside. Combine dry ingredients in a separate bowl. Add eggs, oil, marmalade and orange peel to the cereal mixture. Add mixture to the dry ingredients. Stir to combine. Do not overmix. Fill muffin tins three-quarters full. Bake at 325° for 25 minutes or until they spring back when touched. **Makes 18 muffins.**

CINNAMON BUNDLES

Tamara (Tami) Silvestri
Dallas, TX

A very good friend made these and now it is our family's favorite. My kids love to make these all by themselves. We also eat these at dinnertime. Totally easy to make—totally awesome to eat.

1 package (8-count) refrigerated crescent rolls
8 large marshmallows
½ cup sugar
1 tablespoon cinnamon
½ cup margarine, melted

Roll out and separate dough triangles on a cookie sheet. Brush triangles with butter. Combine sugar and cinnamon. Sprinkle mixture over dough, reserving one-half of mixture. Dip marshmallows in margarine and roll in cinnamon sugar to coat. Place 1 marshmallow in the center of each triangle and pull up sides of dough to cover marshmallow. Press dough together to seal. Place cupcake papers in muffin tin and put each bundle in each of the papers. Bake at 375° for 15 to 20 minutes. **Makes 8.**

PEANUT BUTTER AND JELLY MUFFINS

Mrs. Carol Grimm
Coral Springs, FL

These were always my son Jason's favorite.

Muffins:

2 cups flour
½ cup granulated sugar
2½ teaspoons baking powder
½ cup chunky peanut butter
2 tablespoons butter
2 large eggs, beaten
1 cup buttermilk

Topping:

⅓ cup unsalted toasted peanuts, chopped
¼ cup fruit jelly, melted

Preheat oven to 350° and prepare 12 muffin cups, or 48 mini-muffin cups. Mix flour, sugar and baking powder together. Cut peanut butter and butter into dry mixture until mixture resembles coarse crumbs. In a medium bowl, beat eggs lightly and stir in buttermilk. Add egg-milk mixture to coarse crumb mixture and stir until ingredients are blended. Fill cups two-thirds full. Bake muffins at 350° for 20 to 25 minutes for large muffins, 18 minutes for small muffins.

Combine the topping ingredients while the muffins are baking. As soon as muffins are removed from the oven, brush the tops with topping mixture. **Makes 1 dozen large muffins or 48 mini muffins.**

Serve muffins with a tall glass of cold milk.

CHAPTER TWO

LET'S DO LUNCH

So goes Hollywood's most often heard (however unheeded) invitation. Sometimes lunch on weekends or during summers can mean the family lunching together. But, more often than not lunch goes out the door right after breakfast. If the recipes in this chapter are any indication, InCirclers have pretty sophisticated lunch tastes. Who in the world would trade Southwest Pasta Salad for bologna, or homemade Cheddar Cheese Soup for the canned kind? (No one who's ever faced a lunchroom menu day after day.) With more and more microwave ovens in office kitchens and fewer and fewer expense account lunches allowed, lots of homemade lunches are emerging from attaché cases as well as lunch boxes.

"YOUR FAVORITE MOUSE" PIZZA

Wolfgang Puck
Beverly Hills, CA

The celebrities' celebrity chef sends us this imaginative recipe. But we wonder how many eight-year-olds are regulars at Spago?

1 package active dry or fresh yeast

1 tablespoon honey or sugar

¾ cup warm water (105° to 115° F)

2¾ cups flour

1 teaspoon salt

2 tablespoons olive oil, plus additional for brushing

2 cups Mozzarella cheese, grated

1 Roma tomato, sliced thin (reserve 1 slice)

3 black olives, whole

In small bowl, dissolve yeast and honey in ¼ cup warm water. Next, combine the flour and salt in a mixer fitted with a dough hook. Add 2 tablespoons oil and after absorbed, scrape dissolved yeast into mixture. Add remaining ½ cup water and knead on low speed about 5 minutes.

Turn out onto a board and hand-knead 2 or 3 minutes longer until smooth and firm. Cover with a damp towel, and let rise in a warm place for 30 minutes. (Dough will stretch when lightly pulled.) Divide dough into two balls, about 6 ounces each. Work each ball by pulling down sides and tucking under the bottom of ball. Repeat 4 to 5 times. Then on smooth unfloured surface, roll ball under the palm of your hand until dough is smooth and firm, about 1 minute. Cover with a damp towel and let rest 15 to 20 minutes. At this point, balls may be loosely covered with plastic wrap and refrigerated for 1 to 2 days.

Preheat oven to 450°. Place a pizza stone in the oven for 15 minutes or until very hot. To prepare pizza, place 1 ball of dough on a lightly floured surface. Press down on the center, spreading the dough, or roll with a rolling pin into a circle. Brush lightly with olive oil and set aside. Divide the other ball in half and repeat rolling pin procedure.

To assemble Your Favorite Mouse Pizza, brush the outside top edge of the larger pizza circle with water, and place the small circles where the ears should be. Place 2 cups grated Mozzarella on entire pizza and place tomato slices on small circles for ears, reserving a few for large circle. Cover with remaining cheese. Bake 20 minutes or until crust is golden brown. Remove pizza from pizza stone and place black olives for the eyes and nose. Cut reserved tomato slice in half and use for mouth.

SOLO MIO TRIO PIZZA

Mrs. Marjorie H. Watkins
Glencoe, IL

"Solo Mio" is my pizza crust which I prepare before the three grandchildren arrive for lunch or supper. Each child prepares his own specialty for one-third of the filling. Flavors blend gently during the baking. They devour it in a welcome silence within minutes. The thirteen-year-old makes an excellent pizza crust, and declares my recipe *"easy."*

Astonishing remark from the eight-year-old: *"I know pizza was invented in a Leaning Tower in Italy that's about to fall over flat any day now!"*

Pizza:

1 package regular baking yeast
⅔ cup warm water
½ teaspoon sugar
2 tablespoons olive oil
2¼ cups flour
½ teaspoon salt
1 tablespoon semolina flour or cornmeal

"Trio" Fillings:

¾ cup thick chunky tomato sauce
1 tablespoon basil, chopped
½ cup Mozzarella cheese, shredded
¼ cup frozen spinach, thawed and chopped
1 small red onion, chopped
½ cup white tuna, chopped
¼ cup black olives, drained and sliced
1 package Italian salami, thinly sliced
½ cup Parmesan cheese, grated
Olive oil, for sprinkling

Place yeast in custard cup with warm water and sugar. Set aside for a few minutes until doubled. Place olive oil, salt and flour in large bowl. Add yeast mixture. Process until it forms a ball. Place in olive oil-greased bowl. Cover with plastic wrap. Let rise 1 hour.

Prepare a 14-inch pizza pan by greasing with olive oil and shaking semolina flour into the bottom to cover. Roll out the dough and shape into prepared pan. Spray with olive oil-flavored cooking spray.

Add desired fillings and bake in 400° oven for 25 minutes or until cheese melts and crust begins to brown. **Serves 3.**

Serve pizza with crisp green salad and soft drinks.

POTIONS

Betty Ann Samson
Atlanta, GA

My mother sent me this recipe because, she said, tuna salad and baked potatoes were my favorite foods as a kid.

4 large baking potatoes (Idaho)
1 cup mayonnaise
½ cup Cheddar cheese, grated
¼ cup green pepper, chopped
¼ cup pimientos, chopped
¼ cup onion, chopped
2 cans (6½ ounces each) tuna, drained
2 tablespoons Cheddar cheese, grated
¼ cup mayonnaise
1 egg white, beaten

Bake potatoes at 350° for 1½ hours. Scoop out pulp and mash slightly. Mix one cup mayonnaise with cheese, green pepper, pimientos, onion and tuna and pack into hollowed potato. Heat thoroughly. Combine 2 tablespoons Cheddar cheese, ¼ cup mayonnaise and egg white. Mix thoroughly. Spoon over potatoes and brown lightly. **Serves 4.**

CHICKEN BITS

Sarah Salter Levy
Weston, MA

We serve these whenever anyone comes to visit—they are a fixture on the coffee table. We also bring these to friends who need cheering up.

6 whole boneless, skinless chicken breasts
1 cup seasoned bread crumbs
1 stick margarine, melted
½ cup Parmesan cheese, grated
1 teaspoon garlic salt
1 teaspoon dried basil
1 teaspoon dried thyme
1 teaspoon dried dill

Cut up the breasts into bite-sized pieces. Have the children measure and stir up the bread crumbs, cheese and spices in a big bowl. Dip the chicken pieces into the melted margarine and then into the crumb mixture, coating well. Place the chicken on foil-lined cookie sheets and bake at 400° for 15 minutes. Chicken Bits can be frozen; however, freeze before cooking. Once frozen, bag them in batches and use as needed. **Serves 6.**

GRANDMA'S MACARONI AND CHEESE

Mrs. David Brochstein
Atlanta, GA

This was my mother's version of macaroni and cheese which my children loved. My son now prepares this dish for my grandchildren. Good as a main or side dish and can be prepared with low fat cheese and diet margarine.

"Make mine crunchy! Make mine soft! Make mine anyway, I love it!"

1 package (16 ounces) macaroni, cooked and drained
1 tablespoon margarine
1½ cups low-fat Cheddar cheese, grated
1 can (16 ounces) PROGRESSO® tomato sauce

Pour prepared macaroni into greased 2-quart casserole. Add margarine and cheese to hot macaroni. Allow cheese to melt. Stir thoroughly to coat macaroni. Add tomato sauce and stir.

Place casserole in 350° oven for approximately 1 hour. If you prefer the top crunchy, bake for 45 minutes at 350°, then 15 minutes at 375°. **Serves 6 to 8.**

Serve casserole with fresh coleslaw.

CHEESE ROLL-UPS

Gail Pettigrew
Richardson, TX

This recipe came down through my mother's family. Aunt Opal, my favorite aunt, used to make these on a cold winter's day for all of us kids.

"It's a sandwich—no, it's not a sandwich— who cares, it's great."

1 pound sharp cheese, grated
1 pound medium cheese, grated
1 pound margarine, softened
1 large onion, finely chopped
2½ tablespoons mayonnaise
2½ tablespoons mustard
1 teaspoon garlic powder
1 teaspoon salt
1 teaspoon pepper
½ teaspoon cayenne
Favorite loaf bread, crust removed

Combine cheese, onion and margarine, blend well. Mix in the mayonnaise and mustard, use enough to make a nice spreading consistency. Add the spices and stir. Roll bread slices thin with a rolling pin and spread cheese mixture on bread. Roll up, place on a cookie sheet and bake at 400° until brown. Serve hot. **Makes 5 dozen.**

Note: This spread keeps in the refrigerator for two weeks or in the freezer for six months. It only gets better.

Serve as an appetizer dipped in salsa.

OLD DOGS AND CHILDREN

Willie B. Wilson
Dallas, TX

My three dogs turn up their noses at dog food. So I began making this recipe for them, and when the grandchildren said it smelled so good, I gave them some and they loved it.

"Granny, fix us some of that stuff you fix for the dogs."

1 package (3 ounces) CAMPBELL'S® ramen noodle soup, chicken flavor

Chicken breasts, cooked, boned, and cut into bite-sized pieces

1 can (17 ounces) green beans or peas

Cook noodle soup according to directions. Stir in chicken and vegetables. **Serves 4.**

Serve soup with Momo's Cornbread on page 57.

NORWEGIAN PYTT I PANNE (HASH)

Reidun V. Gann
Beverly Hills, CA

This is a recipe my mother made often, especially when she had leftover meats. Sometimes she used chunk bologna, which I liked better. This is easy to make and can be breakfast, lunch or even dinner.

2 tablespoons butter, melted and divided

2 tablespoons oil, divided

6 medium potatoes, boiled and diced

2 medium onions, diced

4 cups leftover meat, cooked, cut and diced

Salt and pepper, freshly ground, to taste

4 eggs, fried

1 tablespoon parsley, chopped

Heat half the butter and oil and fry the potatoes until golden. Remove and keep warm. Heat remaining butter and oil and cook the onion until transparent. Add the diced meat and cook until browned. Add the potatoes, stirring until completely mixed. Season to taste and decorate with chopped parsley. Top each serving with a fried egg. **Serves 4.**

BIEROX (STUFFED SANDWICHES)

Lynn Kling
Dallas, TX

I was born in a small town settled by German immigrants and this recipe was given to my mother. It is a favorite all year long, but mainly, during the holidays when you are preparing the turkey, etc., you can remove this from the freezer for a quick lunch for everyone.

Here's what my children say:
Geoff: *"BEER OX! UGH! I don't want anything that has beer or ox in it."*
Lindsay: *"Hey, it's not like that—it's great! Give it a try."*

1 loaf BRIDGEFORD® bread, frozen
1 pound lean ground beef
1 medium onion, chopped
½ head cabbage, finely chopped
Salt and pepper to taste

Remove frozen bread from the freezer to thaw. After this has partially thawed, put the ground beef in large iron skillet and gently cook, not browning. After the beef is partially cooked, stir in the onion, and add the seasonings. Add the cabbage and cook until tender. Set aside to cool, removing any grease that may be in the skillet.

Before the bread starts to rise, roll it out on a bread cloth as thin as possible. You will need to work with this bread to get it rolled out. Be sure the ingredients are completely cool by this time or mixture will seep through the dough. Cut the dough into 8 squares, approximately 6 to 7 inches in width. Spoon mixture onto squares, folding up the sides and turning the squares over so that the folded ends are hidden underneath. Bake at 350° until golden brown. The Bierox can be eaten immediately after cooling. Freeze in individual baggies for a quick lunch or snack.
Makes 8.

Serve Bierox with favorite sauce and chips.

CREAMED TUNA ON TOAST

Mary McGee
Norman, OK

My daughter Sandra always requested this when she ate at my friend Nancy's house. She always cut the bread into special shapes such as animals, hearts—and angels if the children were good.

2 tablespoons butter
2 tablespoons flour
1 cup milk
½ cup KRAFT VELVEETA® cheese
¼ teaspoon salt
1 can (6⅛ ounces) tuna
Toast triangles

Melt butter in skillet, stir in flour and gradually stir in milk. Cook until gentle bubbles form. Add grated cheese, salt and tuna. Continue cooking over low heat until cheese melts. Pour tuna over toast triangles. **Serves 2.**

Serve tuna with sliced apples and raisins.

CRUNCHY TUNA MELT

Sandra Mallin
Las Vegas, NV

We tried to vary the standard old boring tuna sandwich.

1 can (6½ ounces) tuna, chopped
2 stalks celery, chopped
2 tablespoons mayonnaise
2 slices Swiss cheese
4 slices white bread
1 egg, beaten
2 cups potato chips, crushed
2 tablespoons butter

Combine tuna, celery and mayonnaise. Place one slice Swiss cheese on each of two slices of bread. Spread half of tuna mixture on top of each and top with remaining bread slices. Dip each sandwich into beaten egg and then into potato chip crumbs. Melt 2 tablespoons butter in skillet. Brown sandwiches on one side, turn and cover skillet. Cook other side until browned and cheese is melted. **Serves 2.**

Serve Crunchy Tuna Melt with carrot sticks and milk.

KEVIN'S TUNA FISH CASSEROLE

Magda Katz
Los Angeles, CA

This recipe is a blend of various family recipes, edited over the years and enjoyed by my three-year-old son, Kevin.

1 package (12 ounces) wide egg noodles
1 can (12½ ounces) water-packed tuna, drained
1 can (2.8 ounces) DURKEE® French-fried onions
1 can (10¾ ounces) cream of mushroom soup, undiluted
6 to 8 slices Muenster or Mozzarella cheese
1 cup low-fat milk

Boil noodles according to package directions and drain. In a large bowl, mix together boiled noodles, tuna, French-fried onions, mushroom soup and milk. Pour half of mixture into a 13x9-inch casserole pan. Place half of cheese slices on top of this portion of mixture. Continue to pour remaining tuna-noodle mixture on top of cheese slices. Complete by layering the remaining cheese slices on top of casserole. Bake at 350° for 30 minutes. **Serves 8 to 10.**

Serve casserole with green salad and rolls.

TUNA BOATS

Kim L. Temple
Dallas, TX

My mother used to make these for us when we were younger. We were able to assist her by cutting the bread and stirring the tuna mixture. It was a nice, hot treat for lunch at home.

4 slices bread
1 can (12½ ounces) tuna
1 cup evaporated skim milk
¼ cup flour
1 teaspoon salt and pepper
1 jar (4½ ounces) mushrooms
½ cup celery, chopped
¼ cup onion, chopped
1 can (16 ounces) baby green peas

Cut crust off of all 4 sides of each slice of bread and press into a muffin/cupcake pan with 4 corners pointing upward. Place pan in oven and broil for 1 minute. Watch carefully for bread to toast and remove from oven and set out to cool. Place remaining ingredients in saucepan at medium heat. Stir tuna mixture until it comes to a slow boil for about 8 minutes. Place each bread boat on plate and, with a soup ladle, spoon tuna mixture into boat and serve. **Serves 4.**

Serve with pear slices and tea.

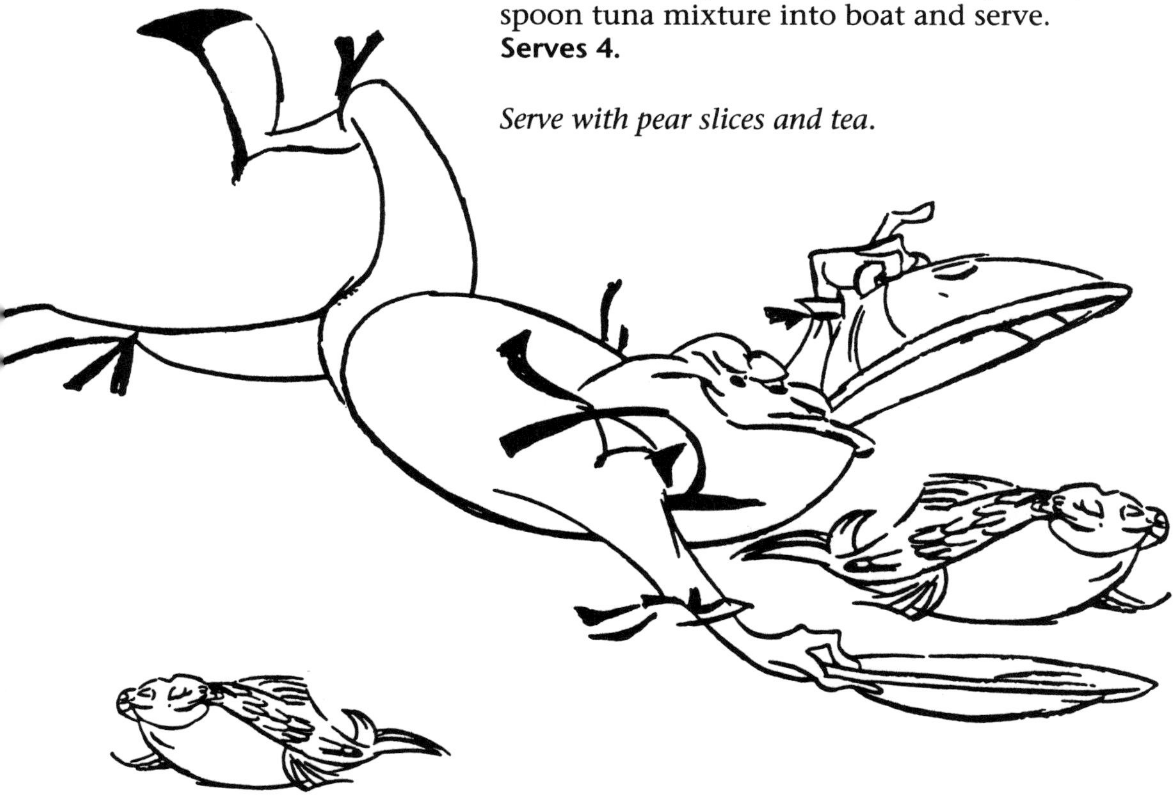

FRENCH TOAST SANDWICHES

Mary A. Bright
Cambridge, MA

Who ever met a child who didn't like French toast? They like this even better!

4 slices Canadian bacon
4 slices Monterey Jack cheese
8 thick slices French or sourdough bread
½ cup eggnog
Powdered sugar, optional
Strawberry preserves or maple syrup (optional)

For each sandwich, stack 1 slice of Canadian-style bacon and 1 slice of cheese between 2 slices of French bread. (As necessary, halve bacon and cheese slices and overlap to fit on the bread.) Dip sandwiches into eggnog, thoroughly coating both sides. Spray a large skillet with nonstick cooking spray and place over medium heat until hot. Add sandwiches. Cook 2½ minutes or until golden. Flip sandwiches and cook until golden. Sift powdered sugar over each sandwich. Serve with strawberry preserves. **Serves 4.**

Serve sandwich with a tall glass of orange juice.

"THE SPENCER GRAY" GOURMET PB&J

Mrs. Wayne Gray
Muncie, IN

My four-year-old Spencer has requested PB&J at some of the finest restaurants throughout the USA and the Caribbean. Amazingly, these fine establishments come up with something. Foxfires Restaurant in Muncie, IN, owned by GARFIELD® creator Jim Davis, requested his recipe and created a sandwich in his honor.

Fresh white bread, crusts removed
Smooth peanut butter
Grape jelly

Spread peanut butter on one slice. Spread grape jelly on the other slice. Place slices together and cut into 4 triangles. **Serves 1.**

Serve sandwiches with carrot sticks and apple slices.

GRILLED PEANUT BUTTER & JELLY SANDWICH

Ronnie and Joyce Milsap
Nashville, TN

Being on the road almost two hundred days a year, our son Todd was raised on tour and he delighted in getting back home and back to the simple snacks and treats you just can't find out there! Ronnie also enjoyed this one with Todd, almost as much as I enjoyed making this old traditional standby for them.

Bread, your choice
Peanut butter
Jelly, your favorite
Margarine

Take 2 pieces of bread, place a generous helping of peanut butter on 1 slice. Add your favorite jelly (we prefer grape) on top and add the other slice of bread. Spread margarine on both the top and bottom of the sandwich; place on a hot griddle on top of stove. Press down lightly until both sides are toasted a golden brown and the peanut butter and jelly are melted together. **Serves 1.**

Serve with a hot bowl of homemade soup, just by itself as a delicious quick snack, or at any meal of the day.

HAPPY SAM SANDWICH

Neiman Marcus
CLASSIC

Happy Sam (and his twin sister, Happy Susie) has made a big hit with every child we know.

1 pimento cheese sandwich
1 cling peach
2 strawberries
2 carrot sticks
1 black olive, chopped

Prepare a pimento cheese sandwich, carefully removing the crust. Cut sandwich in 3 parts, 1 slice from each end about half an inch thick. The remaining middle section will be Sam's body; this should be 2 inches wide. Place the peach at the top of the plate as the head of Sam. Cut black olive to be used as eyes, nose, mouth and ears. Place olive pieces making a face on the peach. Place large part of sandwich underneath the peach, as Sam's body, use the other two slices as arms. The carrot sticks are the legs. Cut the strawberries making the hands and feet. Place in appropriate places. **Serves 1.**

SLOPPY-SLOPPY JOES

Terry Naster
Naperville, IL

This is a weekend favorite of mine; less time is needed to spend in the kitchen leaving me more time with my family who says they are sloppy, and they taste good too!

1 onion, chopped
1 green pepper, chopped
3 tablespoons oil
1 pound lean hamburger
1 bottle (14 ounces) ketchup
3 tablespoons Worcestershire sauce
½ teaspoon mustard
2 tablespoons vinegar
1 teaspoon paprika
1 cup water
1 teaspoon lemon juice
2 tablespoons brown sugar

In a large skillet, combine onion, green pepper and oil. Sauté until tender. Add hamburger and brown, drain off grease. Combine remaining ingredients and simmer for 30 minutes. **Serves 6.**

KIDS' BURRITOS

Sandra Crawford
Mineral Wells, TX

My kids could eat Mexican food three times a day, and this is their favorite. It gets better when reheated the next day. It can be cooked and frozen in smaller quantities. With a salad, this is a complete meal.

When we get a call from Texas A&M saying that the kids are coming in for the weekend, the last thing they say is, *"Mom, could you please make burritos?"*

2 pounds ground beef or ground chicken
1 can RANCH STYLE® beans
1 package dry burrito seasoning mix
1 can (8 ounces) tomato sauce
1½ cups water
1 teaspoon salt
1 teaspoon pepper
½ teaspoon garlic powder
1 small onion, chopped
1 can (4 ounces) green chilies, chopped
2 to 3 cups grated cheese
2 dozen flour tortillas

Brown ground beef or chicken and drain. Add all other ingredients except cheese and tortillas. Mix well and simmer 15 minutes. Spoon mixture in center of each tortilla, top with a tablespoon of cheese and roll up. Place burritos, seam side down, in a greased 3-quart casserole. Sprinkle with remaining cheese. Spoon remaining meat sauce mixture over burritos. Cover with foil and bake at 400° for 30 to 40 minutes.

Serves 8 to 12.

Serve burritos with chips and salsa.

OVEN-FRIED QUESADILLAS

Amanda Shams
Atlanta, GA

I like to make these in the springtime when my family and I can eat outside among the aromatic magnolias and dogwoods. My girls absolutely adore these different lunchtime treats.

2½ cups Monterey Jack cheese, melted
1 jar (6 ounces) marinated artichoke hearts, drained and chopped
1 can (2¼ ounces) sliced ripe olives, drained
⅔ cup picante sauce
½ cup toasted almonds, chopped
¼ cup loosely packed cilantro, chopped
8 (8-inch) flour tortillas
3 tablespoons butter or margarine, melted

Preheat oven to 350°. Combine cheese, artichokes, olives, picante sauce and almonds in a large bowl; mix well. Brush 1 side of 4 tortillas with butter and place buttered side down on baking sheet. Place 1 cup cheese mixture on each of 4 tortillas and spread to within ¾ inch of edge; top each with remaining tortillas, pressing firmly. Brush top of tortillas with butter. Bake at 350° about 10 minutes or until tops are lightly browned. Remove from oven and let stand 3 to 5 minutes. Cut each quesadilla into 8 wedges. **Serves 8.**

Serve quesadillas with additional picante sauce and lime wedges.

SMOKED TURKEY ENCHILADAS

Marilyn J. Chapman
Seabrook, TX

A great recipe for a family who simply cannot get enough Mexican food.

2 dozen tomatillos, husked, cooked and drained
1 pint sour cream
2 teaspoons ground cumin
2 cloves garlic, minced
1 dozen corn tortillas
1 cup smoked turkey, chopped
½ cup green onions, chopped
1½ cups Monterey Jack cheese, grated
2 tablespoons cilantro, finely chopped

Gently simmer tomatillos in water until soft enough to put into food processor. Combine sour cream, cumin and garlic in food processor. Soak tortillas in this green sauce until soft enough to roll. Place 2 tablespoons turkey into each tortilla along with green onions. Roll and place into 9x12-inch glass baking dish. After all enchiladas are rolled and in baking dish, pour green sauce over the enchiladas, top with cheese and remaining green onion. Bake at 350° for 15 minutes or until bubbly. Sprinkle with cilantro and serve. Use fresh tortillas; they are easier to handle. **Serves 6 to 8.**

Note: Be sure to soak tortillas in green sauce so they will be pliable.

Serve enchiladas with Spanish rice and beans.

SOUTHWEST PASTA SALAD

Judith H. Willers
Agoura Hills, CA

Several years ago, I developed this recipe for my sons Erik and Brent who were lacrosse players. They wanted something good but not heavy and that would give them the right kind of energy for a very physical game.

1 package (16 ounces) bow tie pasta
1 medium red onion, chopped
1 red bell pepper, chopped
1 yellow bell pepper, chopped
1 package (10 ounces) frozen corn, thawed
1 bottle (8 ounces) Italian salad dressing
1 jar (16 ounces) mild picante sauce or salsa
1¼ cups Monterey Jack cheese, shredded

Cook pasta according to package directions. Drain and cool. Add onion, peppers and corn. In a separate bowl, combine Italian dressing and picante sauce and pour over pasta. Mix well. Add cheese, mix and refrigerate. **Serves 6 to 8.**

Note: Do not overcook pasta because the acidity from the dressing will cause it to break down.

Add ¾ cup cooked and cubed turkey to pasta dish for a complete meal.

TEX-MEX SALAD

Judi Amore
Highwood, IL

Instead of tacos (a favorite of my kids), this is a great chilled salad—very much like a taco, easy to make and fun for them to eat.

3 medium ripe avocados, mashed, or 2 packages (6 ounces each) frozen avocado dip
2 tablespoons lemon juice
½ teaspoon salt
¼ teaspoon pepper
1 cup sour cream
½ cup mayonnaise
1 package taco seasoning
1 large bunch green onions, chopped
½ head iceberg lettuce, chopped
3 medium ripe tomatoes, cored, seeded
1 jar (6 ounces) ripe pitted olives, chopped
2 cans (11 ounces each) bean dip
1 cup (8 ounces) Cheddar cheese, shredded

Combine avocados, lemon juice, salt and pepper and set aside. Mix together the sour cream, mayonnaise and taco seasoning. Layer salad in order on a large 12-inch dish: onions, lettuce, tomatoes and olives. Spread bean dip, avocado mix and sour cream mix over the top and cover with shredded cheese. **Serves 4 to 6.**

Serve salad with favorite tortilla chips.

CHINESE CHICKEN SALAD

Jean S. Wong
San Francisco, CA

This recipe has been passed down from two generations of the Wong clan. Our generation now makes it for our parents and grandparents as well as our children. Not only is it a do-ahead dish, but the children participate and enjoy shredding the chicken while watching television.

"Mom, we like that salad that has everything in it that's good for you, and we helped!"

Chicken Salad:

10 chicken breasts, baked, skinned and shredded
1 bottle (3 ounces) sesame seeds
1 package (8 ounces) slivered almonds
2 heads iceberg lettuce, shredded
2 bunches green onions, diced
2 bunches cilantro, stemmed and chopped

Dressing:

¾ cup BERTOLLI® red wine vinegar
5 tablespoons sesame oil
½ cup plus 2 tablespoons sugar
5 teaspoons salt
1 teaspoon pepper
1¼ cups safflower oil

Bake chicken breasts at 350° for about 45 minutes. Allow to cool. Remove skin and shred. Brown sesame seeds and slivered almonds separately in a pan on the stove. (Please watch carefully as the sesame seeds brown quickly).

Combine all salad ingredients in a large bowl. Combine all the dressing ingredients. Pour just enough dressing over the salad to lightly coat. Allow guests to add more to their own plates if they wish. **Serves 10.**

Serve salad with bread sticks.

VALENCIAN CHICKEN SALAD

Myrna Elliott
Laguna Beach, CA

An old Castilian family recipe handed down from four generations of Spaniards.

6 chicken breasts, cooked and shredded

1 whole onion, halved

6 large potatoes, peeled and cubed

6 eggs, hard-boiled

2 jars (4 ounces each) red pimiento peppers, chopped

1 can (6 ounces) pitted green olives, chopped

2 bunches green onions, chopped

2 cups mayonnaise

Lemon pepper to taste

Salt to taste

In a large pot, place chicken breasts, onion halves and enough water to cover. Boil until tender. Cool, bone and shred chicken. Place potatoes and water in separate pot and boil until tender. Cool. Hard-boil eggs. After eggs have cooled, peel and chop. In a large bowl, add potatoes, eggs, chicken, green onions, red pimientos and olives. Stir in mayonnaise, lemon pepper and salt to taste. **Serves 6 to 8.**

Serve salad with baguettes or warm rolls.

BLUSHING BUNNY

Mrs. Arthur L. Owen
Dallas, TX

The recipe came from my mother Mrs. Ralph A. Belknap, Sr. This was a *"some Sunday night"* favorite at home when the cook had left.

½ pound yellow or extra sharp Cheddar cheese, grated
1 can tomato soup, undiluted
Saltine crackers

In a medium saucepan, combine soup and cheese. Heat until cheese is melted. Stir frequently or use a double boiler. Pour over saltine crackers. **Serves 2.**

Serve with fresh fruit and milk.

CHEDDAR CHEESE SOUP

Dr. & Mrs. Marcus Adams
Norman, OK

During the 1970s we took our children to the C-Lazy-U Ranch, (Colorado) where we enjoyed many memorable meals. Cheddar Cheese Soup was an all-time favorite.

4 tablespoons butter, melted
½ cup carrots, diced
½ cup green pepper, diced
½ cup onion, diced
½ cup celery, diced
⅓ cup flour
1 quart chicken broth
1½ cups Cheddar cheese, grated
1½ cups sharp Cheddar cheese, grated
4 cups whole milk
Salt and white pepper to taste

In soup pot, melt butter. Add vegetables and simmer until tender but not browned. Whisk in flour and cook, stirring, 1 minute. Add broth and cook, stirring, until thickened. Turn heat to low. Add cheese and cook, stirring, until melted. Stir in milk and bring to a simmer. Season to taste. **Serves 8.**

Serve soup with shredded cheese and oyster crackers.

TAMALE SOUP

Jane Hoffmann
Dallas, TX

Our grandchildren know they're deep in the heart of Texas when they are served this soup. It's No. 1 on their list of requests when they visit during the holidays.

2 tablespoons olive oil
1 pound ground beef
1 medium onion, chopped
1 green pepper, chopped
1 can (16 ounces) stewed tomatoes
2 cans (15 ounces each) pinto beans, undrained
1 can (16 ounces) creamed corn
1 can (10¾ ounces) beef bouillon
2 jars or cans (16 ounces each) tamales, cut to 1 inch

Heat olive oil in skillet. Add beef, onions and green pepper and brown. Add remaining ingredients, except tamales, and simmer for 1 hour. Add tamales before serving. Better the second day, as time improves the flavor. **Serves 6.**

MOMO'S CORN BREAD

Mrs. W. Humphrey Bogart
Dallas, TX

From my grandmother who got it from her grandmother who came to Texas in a covered wagon from Tennessee.

Kids say: *"Yummy! Especially with soup."*

½ cup shortening, melted
2 eggs
4 tablespoons sugar
1 cup flour
2 teaspoons baking powder
½ teaspoon soda
¾ teaspoon salt
⅔ cup yellow cornmeal
1 cup buttermilk

Melt shortening in 9-inch iron skillet (must be an iron skillet) while preheating oven to 400°. In a separate bowl, beat eggs and add sugar. Stir. Sift together dry ingredients. Alternately add sifted dry ingredients with buttermilk. Pour batter into prepared skillet. Bake at 400° for 30 minutes. **Serves 8.**

Serve cornbread with tomato soup.

CHAPTER THREE

EVERYONE'S ENTITLED TO GRAZING RIGHTS

It seems the whole world or at least most Americans has taken up grazing on snack foods. Sometimes it's hard to tell where one meal ends and another begins. It's the way kids have always preferred to eat, and now grown-ups munch breakfast on the way to work and nibble as we talk on the speakerphone. We found InCirclers full of good ideas for food that can be eaten out of hand and on the run. If you thought milk and cookies were the be-all and end-all in snacks, wait until you try Watermelon Cookies or Apple Cider Corn Bread. Feel free to gnosh, by gosh.

GOOD-GOOD CARAMEL CORN

Dr. Deborah (Debbe)
H. Cawthon
Dallas, TX

This was a favorite recipe of my mother's and I've been making it for years. My twenty-three-year-old son loves it. It will keep ten days to two weeks—but never lasts that long!

2 sticks butter
2 cups brown sugar
½ cup KARO® syrup
1 teaspoon salt
1 teaspoon soda
¼ teaspoon cream of tartar
6 quarts popcorn, popped
1 cup pecans, peanuts or almonds

In a double boiler, cook the butter, sugar and syrup until the hard-ball stage. Add salt, soda, and cream of tartar to cooked syrup mixture. Place popcorn and nuts on a large cookie sheet and drizzle with the syrup mixture. Mix well. Put in oven and bake at 225° for 1 hour. Stir once while baking. **Makes 6 quarts.**

Note: If desired, maple flavoring can be substituted by using maple syrup.

Serve caramel corn with chilled soda.

STRAWBERRY SHORT STAKES

Aric Bendorf
Santa Monica, CA

As a thirty-one-year-old father of three girls, I try to give them snacks that will please their sweet tooths and yet provide nutrition. We have fun making these together. My daughter Mindy named them because they taste like her favorite dessert, strawberry shortcake.

1 quart freshly squeezed orange juice, strained to remove pulp and seeds
2 cups fresh strawberries, sliced
2 tablespoons unpasteurized honey

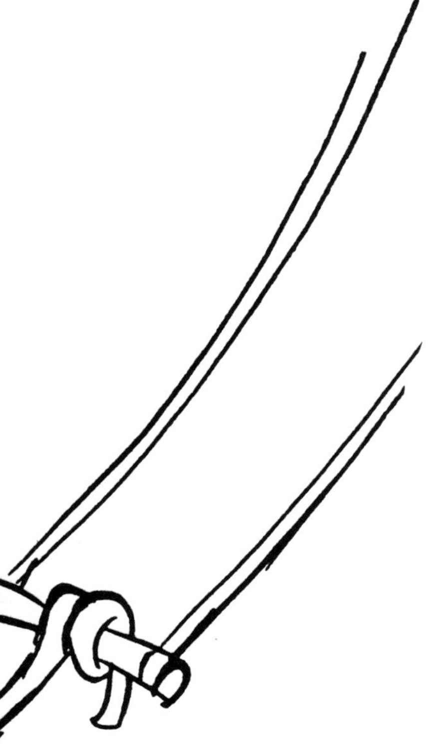

Remember that children are helping you prepare this. Therefore it is a very good idea to use only plastic utensils and plastic containers. If fresh strawberries are unavailable, frozen whole strawberries may be substituted. However they must be warmed to room temperature and require slightly more honey.

Squeeze oranges and pour strained juice into a 2-quart pitcher. Place sliced strawberries into a blender and liquefy. Slowly blend in honey until entire mixture is a free-running syrup. Force mixture through a strainer, to remove pulp and seeds, then pour into the freshly squeezed orange juice. Mix thoroughly with a large spoon. Pour into freezer molds and freeze overnight. **Serves 8.**

Serve with plenty of napkins!

MOM'S GRANOLA

Sharon Schwartz
Houston, TX

This is a healthy snack I discovered ten years ago. It has gone to school in lunch boxes many times, and now I send it to my kids at the University of Texas before every midterm and final.

¾ cup brown sugar, firmly packed
¼ cup honey
¼ cup water
1 teaspoon salt
½ cup margarine
3 cups old-fashioned rolled oats, uncooked
1 cup sliced almonds, toasted
1 cup wheat germ
¼ cup sesame seeds
1 cup dried apricots, chopped
½ cup raisins

Combine brown sugar, honey, water and salt in electric skillet. Cook at 260°, stirring constantly, for 5 minutes, or until margarine melts and mixture is slightly thickened. Stir in oats, almonds, wheat germ and sesame seeds. Cook, stirring frequently, for 10 minutes or until oats are lightly toasted. Stir in apricots and raisins. Pour mixture into a 15½x10½x 1-inch jelly roll pan, spreading to the edges of pan. Press mixture down slightly, using spatula. Let stand 30 minutes. Break into small pieces. Store in an airtight container. **Serves 6 to 8.**

Serve granola with sliced apples.

FRUIT SHAKE

Janie Friend
San Francisco, CA

I used to work for Nathan Pritikin (Pritikin Institute) in Santa Monica, so I know that good food that's good for you is double good. My kids say the best part is that they choose what goes in it and it's different every time.

1 cup mixed fruit
1 ripe banana
1 cup plain yogurt or sweetened if you prefer
1 cup carrot juice
1 cup fruit juice
1½ cups ice

Use a blender to mix together all ingredients, except ice. Add ice at last minute and blend. Pour into tall iced glasses. Add straws and garnish each with a strawberry or apple slice. **Serves 4.**

Serve shake with bran muffins.

TEA CAKE RECIPE

Mrs. Clinton Davis
Many, LA

Back in my day (the twenties and thirties) children did not have many store-bought cookies. This recipe was made by a neighbor of my mother's and was a particular favorite with all the neighborhood children.

1½ cups sugar
½ cup shortening
2 eggs
½ teaspoon lemon extract
½ teaspoon vanilla extract
½ cup buttermilk
1 teaspoon soda
4 cups flour

Cream the sugar and shortening. Add eggs one at a time and beat well. Stir in flavorings. Add buttermilk, soda and flour alternately to make a stiff dough. Chill. When dough is firm, roll out on floured paper. Cut into desired shapes and bake on greased cookie sheet at 350° for 8 minutes until very lightly browned. **Makes 3 dozen.**

Serve cakes with hot tea and lemon curd.

OATMEAL CHERRY CHIPPERDOOS

Joyce M. Konigsberg
Ross, CA

Every Memorial Day, our neighborhood stages a parade. The kids decorate their bikes and tricycles and we all have a great time. Even though my son is now a teenager, our house is still a popular gathering place for younger children. I always try to keep cookies on hand. This is the favorite.

1 cup butter
1 cup dark brown sugar
½ cup sugar
2 large eggs
1 teaspoon vanilla extract
1½ cups flour
½ teaspoon salt
½ teaspoon baking soda
½ teaspoon baking powder
1 teaspoon cinnamon
2 cups old-fashioned oatmeal, uncooked
1 cup cherries, drained and chopped
1 cup miniature chocolate chips

Preheat oven to 350°. Cream the butter and sugars and beat until well blended. Add the eggs and vanilla and beat until light and fluffy. Mix together the flour, salt, baking soda, baking powder and cinnamon. Add flour mixture to the butter mixture and beat until well blended. Stir in the oatmeal, cherries and miniature chocolate chips. Drop the batter by tablespoonfuls onto lightly greased cookie sheets and bake 12 minutes or until the edges turn brown. Cool in the pan for a minute, then place on racks to cool completely.

Note: Dried apricots may be substituted for the cherries. Butterscotch chips may be substituted for chocolate chips. **Makes 4 dozen.**

Serve cookies with frozen vanilla yogurt.

COWBOY COOKIES

Dana Hagen
Hillsboro Beach, FL

I don't know why these are called *"cowboy cookies,"* but I've been making them for years, ever since I got the recipe when we lived in Columbus, Ohio. It's traveled all over the country with us—we've lived in a lot of places.

2 cups flour, sifted
1 teaspoon baking soda
½ teaspoon salt
½ teaspoon baking powder
1 cup shortening
1 cup sugar
1 cup brown sugar, packed
2 eggs
1 teaspoon vanilla extract
1¾ cups rolled oats
1 package (6 ounces) milk chocolate chips

Mix flour, soda, salt and baking powder and set aside. Cream together shortening and sugars. Add eggs and vanilla, and mix well. Add flour mixture and mix well. Stir in oats and chocolate chips. Drop by spoonfuls onto greased cookie sheets. Bake at 350° for 12 to 15 minutes. **Makes 5 dozen.**

Serve cookies with chocolate ice cream.

PEANUT BUTTER SQUARES

Ann Denison
Ft. Lauderdale, FL

Peanut Butter has been a favorite of my sons Chris (age 24), Bob (age 16) and Ed (age 13). It was copied from a dessert served at a fishing club in the Keys. It has become a family dessert and snack for twenty years now.

6 ounces graham cracker crumbs
1 cup peanut butter
½ pound margarine
3½ cups powdered sugar
2 cups chocolate chips

Butter a 9x13-inch pan. In a bowl, combine crumbs, peanut butter and sugar. Blend until smooth. Press into buttered pan. In a double boiler, melt chips over hot water. Spread chocolate over crumb mixture. Let cool. Cut into squares to serve. **Serves 10 to 12.**

Serve squares with cold milk.

COOKIE ON A STICK

Chef Mark Baker
Four Seasons Hotel
Chicago, IL

2 cups light brown sugar
½ cup sugar
Pinch of salt
1 teaspoon vanilla extract
5 eggs
3 cups cake flour
3 cups chocolate chips
36 wooden sticks
1 cup white chocolate
1 tablespoon cream

Cream sugars, salt, vanilla extract and butter. Add eggs and blend well. Add flour and stir to combine. Fold in chocolate chips. Using a small ice cream scoop, place cookie dough on a sheet pan that has been lined with parchment paper. Insert stick into the side of the scoop before baking. Bake at 375° for 10 to 12 minutes. When cookies have cooled, place white chocolate and cream in a microwavable container and microwave for 40 seconds on high to melt chocolate. Remove and stir, making sure all is melted. Place chocolate in a pastry bag with a small tip and pipe a smiling face on each cookie. **Makes 3 dozen.**

PINK PIG COOKIES

Mrs. Guy Edward Moman
Tuscaloosa, AL

I make these often to fill pig cookie jars or tins, and I always tell the recipient that the container is the Mama Pig and they must return her or there will not be any more baby pigs. I even made a batch for a friend who had a heart valve replaced with a pig valve. Big hit!

1 cup butter, softened
2 cups sugar
2 eggs, beaten
¼ cup milk
3 teaspoons vanilla extract
4 teaspoons baking powder
½ teaspoon salt
¼ teaspoon nutmeg
4 cups flour
Red food coloring

Beat butter, sugar, eggs, milk and vanilla until well blended. Combine flour, baking powder, salt and nutmeg and add to egg mixture half a cup at a time and blend after each addition. Gradually add food coloring while blending until pink color is obtained. (I usually use several drops of liquid color.) Divide dough into 6 portions, wrap in plastic and refrigerate at least 1 hour. Dough will stay fresh up to one week in refrigerator or two months in the freezer.

Preheat oven to 375°. Remove one portion of enough to roll. Place dough on lightly floured surface and roll to a quarter inch thick. Cut dough into pig shapes. Yield will depend on size you desire to cut shapes. Place on ungreased cookie sheets and bake 8 minutes or until edges are brown. Remove from pans to cool. Using a toothpick, dot food coloring on pigs for eyes. **Makes 3 dozen.**

Serve cookies with cold chocolate milk.

WATERMELON COOKIES

Susan M. Miller
Chesterfield, MO

Although they are made from a basic sugar cookie dough, they seem to have a taste of summer sunshine in every bite. My children request them for birthday parties, swimming parties, picnics, etc.

6 tablespoons margarine
⅓ cup vegetable shortening
¾ cup sugar
1 egg
1 teaspoon vanilla extract
1 tablespoon orange juice or milk
Red food coloring
3 cups flour
1½ teaspoons baking powder
½ teaspoon salt
¼ cup miniature chocolate chips
1 egg white
1 tablespoon water
Green sugar: ½ cup sugar combined with drop of green food coloring

In mixer, beat margarine, shortening and sugar. Add egg, vanilla, orange juice and enough food coloring to make dough bright pink. Sift together flour, baking powder and salt. Add to first mixture and blend thoroughly. Chill dough until easy to handle.

On floured surface, roll dough until a quarter inch thick. Cut dough with a 2-inch cookie cutter. Cut each of the 2-inch circles in half and place on ungreased cookie sheet. Press 6 to 7 miniature chocolate chips into each unbaked cookie, not too close to circle edge. Bake in 350° oven for 8 to 10 minutes. DO NOT BROWN. Cool on rack.

Mix egg white and water. When cookies are cool, roll rounded edge through the egg white mixture and then through green sugar. Dry on racks. If you freeze cookies prior to rolling them in the sugar, you will keep the edges from getting soggy. **Makes 4 dozen.**

Serve cookies with vanilla yogurt.

CARAMEL CRISPY-CHOCOLATE BARS

Mrs. Cissy Brottman
Northfield, IL

This is a fun recipe that I have made with my children and grandchildren because it is simple and quick. The kids love unwrapping (and eating) all the caramels; and since the toppings are done in the microwave, the children can participate safely.

"We don't know if it's more fun eating them or making them."

Crust:

1¼ cups flour
½ cup powdered sugar
½ cup cold butter

Filling:

1 package (14 ounces) vanilla caramels
⅓ cup evaporated milk
¼ cup butter

Topping:

1 package (6 ounces) semisweet chocolate chips
3 tablespoons shortening
¾ cup crispy rice cereal

Crust: Heat oven to 350°. In medium bowl, combine flour and powdered sugar. Using mixer, pastry blender or fork, cut in butter until crumbly. Lightly press mixture in ungreased 13x9-inch pan. Bake at 350° for 10 to 12 minutes or until light brown.

Filling: In a microwave-safe dish, combine caramels, evaporated milk and ¼ cup butter. Microwave on high for 3 minutes, or until mixture is smooth, stirring 2 or 3 times during cooking. Spread over baked crust.

Topping: In a microwave-safe dish, combine chocolate chips and shortening. Microwave on high for 1¼ minutes or until melted, stirring once halfway through cooking. Stir until smooth. Stir in cereal. Carefully spread over filling. Cool. Cut into bars. **Makes 18 bars.**

Serve bars with cold milk.

GOOEY BARS

Mrs. John H. Connell
Newport Beach, CA

This comes from northern Michigan where all the ladies baked and baked. These are moist and keep that way as long as you wish. My nine children couldn't wait to come home to Gooey Bars.

Cake:

1 package yellow cake mix, not with pudding
1 stick butter, melted
1 egg
1 teaspoon vanilla extract
2 cups pecans, chopped

Icing:

1 package (8 ounces) cream cheese, softened
2 eggs
1 package (16 ounces) powdered sugar, reserve ½ cup
1 teaspoon vanilla extract

Combine cake mix, butter and 1 egg, mix well and add vanilla. Fold in pecans. Pat into buttered 9x13-inch pan. For icing, beat cream cheese and add 2 eggs, one at a time. Add vanilla. Add powdered sugar and mix well. Pour on top of first mixture. Sift remaining powdered sugar over top. Bake at 350° for 45 minutes. Cool and cut into small squares. **Serves 12.**

MUD HEN BARS

Mrs. Dale Granacki
Fort Worth, TX

½ cup margarine
1 cup sugar
1 egg, whole
2 eggs, separated
1½ cups flour
1 teaspoon baking soda
¼ teaspoon salt
1 cup pecans, chopped
½ cup semisweet chocolate chips
1 cup miniature marshmallows
1 cup light brown sugar

Cream margarine and sugar. Beat in 1 whole egg and 2 egg yolks. Stir in flour, baking soda and salt. Mix well. Spread into 9x13-inch pan which has been coated with nonstick cooking spray. Sprinkle with pecans, chocolate chips and marshmallows. Beat remaining 2 egg whites until stiff, then fold in brown sugar. Spread over top of cake. Bake at 350° for 30 to 40 minutes. Cut into squares. **Serves 10 to 12.**

MIMI'S PEANUT BUTTER BROWNIES

Pamela K. Baxter
New York, NY

My grandmother, Mimi, used to make this recipe for me, and now I make it for my son who now has children of his own. I can't wait until they are old enough to see if the peanut butter craving will continue.

2 eggs
1 cup butter
¾ cup light brown sugar
¼ cup crunchy peanut butter
1 teaspoon vanilla extract
2 tablespoons butter, softened
1⅓ cups flour
2 teaspoons baking powder
¼ teaspoon salt
¼ cup salted peanuts, chopped

Butter a 9x9-inch pan. Preheat oven to 350°. Combine eggs, butter, brown sugar, peanut butter, vanilla and butter in a bowl and beat thoroughly. Sift together the flour, baking powder and salt. Stir into butter mixture. Spread in the prepared pan. Sprinkle peanuts over the top and press in lightly. Bake 30 minutes. Cut into squares while warm. **Serves 16.**

Serve brownies with chocolate sauce.

DOUGH BOYS

Jo-Ann M. Brown
Bronxville, NY

These little fried breads are a family tradition and have been handed down over many generations beginning with my great-great-great grandmother in Sicily. *"More Dough Boys, Mom!"* say my children.

1 cup water
8 tablespoons butter
Salt to taste
1 tablespoon sugar
1 cup flour
4 eggs
Corn oil for frying
¼ cup granulated sugar

Put water in a saucepan and add butter, salt and sugar. Bring to boil. Add the flour all at once, mixing with a wooden spoon to form a ball. Remove from heat and add the eggs one at a time until they are well blended.

Heat oil in a skillet. Using a tablespoon, drop the batter into oil one by one. Cook evenly for 4 to 5 minutes until crisp and golden brown. Drain on paper towels and then toss or sprinkle them in the sugar. Serve immediately.
Makes 3 to 4 dozen.

Call the kids and have milk or cocoa ready.

CLARA HALL'S BUTTERMILK CAKE

Vicki Farina
Racine, WI

Clara Hall lived on the hill above my grandmother and once brought this to one of our family gatherings. Now I make it every year for my twelve-year-old son Sam on his birthday.

2 cups sugar
1¼ cups vegetable oil
6 eggs, separated
1 teaspoon soda
1 cup buttermilk
3 cups flour
1 teaspoon salt
1 teaspoon baking powder
1 cup sugar

Sauce for Cake:

1 stick butter, melted
½ cup sugar
3 tablespoons flour
2 cups milk
1 teaspoon vanilla or almond extract

Cream together 2 cups sugar, vegetable oil and egg yolks. Dissolve soda in buttermilk and beat until foamy. Mix with sugar mixture. Sift the flour, salt and baking powder together and add to the sugar mixture. In a separate glass mixing bowl, beat egg whites until peaks form. Beat in remaining 1 cup sugar. Gently fold egg whites into flour mixture. Do not beat once egg whites are folded in. Grease and flour pan. Bake in a 9x13-inch pan at 350° for 1 hour or until toothpick comes out clean.

Sauce For Cake: In a medium-sized saucepan combine butter, sugar and flour over low heat. Add milk and cook until thickened. (If you get it too thick, add more milk.) Add vanilla or almond flavorings or any flavorings you prefer. Serve warm over cake. **Serves 12 to 16.**

Serve cake with vanilla ice cream or yogurt.

DRIVE ME BANANAS BREAD

Alison Dennis
Fort Collins, CO

After living in Indonesia and Malaysia for years, my family became used to picking bananas off the trees. Now that we live in Colorado, they love them in this bread and say *"it's banana-licious!"*

2 cups bread flour
½ teaspoon baking powder
½ teaspoon soda
½ teaspoon salt
¾ cup sugar
¼ cup butter
1 egg
¾ cup bananas, mashed
3 tablespoons sour milk or buttermilk

Sift together flour, baking powder, soda and salt. Cream sugar and butter until light. Add egg and beat well. Beat in mashed bananas. Alternately stir in one-third of butter mixture and one-third of milk into the flour mixture until blended and all ingredients are used. Place batter in greased 8x4-inch loaf pan. Bake at 350° for 1 hour. **Serves 12.**

Serve bread toasted, with chocolate sauce.

APPLE CIDER CORN BREAD

Elizabeth E. Solender &
Gary L. Scott
Dallas, TX

We served corn bread and apple sauce to our nieces and nephews and watched as they spread the apple sauce on the bread. This gave me the idea to experiment until I came up with this perfect combination of apple chunks, apple cider and spices blended into the corn bread. To the best of my knowledge, it's an original.

1 cup yellow cornmeal
1 cup flour
3 tablespoons sugar
1 teaspoon ground cinnamon
1 teaspoon salt
4 teaspoons baking powder
¼ teaspoon ground cloves
¼ teaspoon mace or nutmeg
2 Granny Smith apples cored, peeled and cubed
1 cup apple cider
¼ cup cooking oil
1 egg

Preheat the oven to 400° and grease a 9x9x2-inch baking pan. Stir together first 8 dry ingredients. Core and peel the 2 apples, then cut them into half-inch cubes. Place the apple cubes into the cup of apple cider. Measure the oil, then add the egg to the oil and beat lightly with a fork. Add the apple cider with apple cubes and the oil and egg to the dry ingredients and mix with a wooden spoon until smooth. Turn the mixture into the greased pan and bake in a 400° oven for 25 to 35 minutes. **Serves 8 to 9.**

Serve corn bread with apple butter.

PEPPERONI CHEESE WHEEL

Joy Daley
Dallas, TX

A good friend of mine who is quite the social butterfly in Wichita, Kansas gave me this recipe. She serves it at almost every party and always at the party she gives whenever we visit Wichita.

1 package (8 ounces) cream cheese
½ teaspoon garlic powder
½ teaspoon onion powder
1 teaspoon chives, chopped
1¼ cups Muenster cheese, shredded
1 package (3½ ounces) pepperoni, finely chopped
1 tablespoon half-and-half
Ground red pepper seeds
2 teaspoons paprika

In a medium-sized bowl, soften cream cheese with electric mixer. Blend thoroughly, adding garlic, onion, chives, Muenster cheese, pepperoni and half-and-half. Shape cheese into a ball and then flatten into a wheel shape. On waxed paper, combine red pepper and paprika. Roll cheese wheel in spices to completely cover. Wrap and refrigerate. Freezes up to three months. **Serves 8 to 10.**

Serve cheese wheel with wheat crackers or bagel chips.

ARKANSAS DIP

Mrs. Charles M. Kirkland
Dallas, TX

Recipe of son and daughter-in-law, Ron and Fran Box of Blue Ridge, Texas. A hit at family gatherings before mealtime.

1 can ROTEL® tomatoes, chopped
¼ cup milk
1 package (3 ounces) lemon gelatin
1 package (8 ounces) cream cheese
½ cup bell peppers, combined red and green, chopped
3 stalks celery, finely chopped
¼ cup onion, finely chopped
½ cup pecans, chopped
½ cup MIRACLE WHIP®

Combine tomatoes, milk, gelatin and cream cheese in sauce pan, stir until melted. Fold in remaining ingredients. Chill overnight. **Serves 6.**

Serve dip with potato chips, corn chips or crackers.

BEEF JERKY

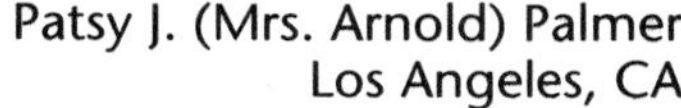

Patsy J. (Mrs. Arnold) Palmer
Los Angeles, CA

I have four sons who loved this recipe when they were in school. We still love it, and it goes with us on cookouts and hikes and has traveled with us from Los Angeles to London.

1 (16 ounces) flank steak, trimmed
½ cup soy sauce
Garlic salt
Lemon pepper

Slicing with the grain, cut steak lengthwise into strips no more than half an inch thick. Toss with soy sauce. Arrange strips in a single layer on a wire rack in a shallow pan. Sprinkle with the garlic salt and lemon pepper. Bake at 150° to 175° overnight or for 10 to 12 hours.
Serves 6 to 8.

Serve jerky with soft drinks.

STUFFED FRANKS

Mrs. Ellyn-Mae G. Friedman
Norfolk, VA

I am Bubbie (Grandmother) to children six months to seven years of age. While they will honor traditions like matzo ball soup for Passover and potato pancakes for Hanukkah, this recipe is always a hit.

2 cups potatoes, mashed
½ cup low-fat yellow cheese, grated
2 tablespoons onion, grated
8 to 10 all-beef kosher frankfurters
2 tablespoons yellow mustard
Paprika
Margarine

Mix the mashed potatoes with the cheese and onions. Split the franks and spread with yellow mustard. Fill cavity with the potato mixture. Sprinkle the potatoes with paprika and dot with margarine, if desired. Place on broiler rack about three inches from the heat. Broil 10 minutes or until golden brown. **Serves 5.**

Serve with homemade French-fried potatoes.

FRUIT CHARACTERS: "PUPPY DOG SALAD"

Karen Sheetz
Newport Beach, CA

As a teacher of children's cooking classes, I have always included this recipe in the birthday party menus. It's quick, it's easy and it's entirely edible.

1 lettuce leaf
1 pear half, canned
1 prune
1 maraschino cherry
1 raisin
2 mandarin orange slices

Wash lettuce leaf, shake off water and lay on a plate. Place pear half on the lettuce leaf so that the large end is higher than the small end and the rounded side faces up. Place the prune on the large round side for the ear. Place the maraschino cherry at the end of the small side for the nose. Place raisin in front of prune for the eye. Place the 2 mandarin orange slices along the bottom of the pear to look like a collar.
Serves 1.

Serve salad with hot dogs and buns.

CHAPTER FOUR

EVERYBODY, SIT DOWN FOR DINNER

What happens when romantic dinners for two become dinners for three, four, five . . . ? That's when you say *au revoir* to paté and squab under glass. Good family dinner menus are much more likely to revolve around hearty casseroles and stews, barbecued meats and lots of old-fashioned chicken dishes. In our survey of InCircle dinner recipes, we found a distinct trend: almost anything with ground beef, cheese and tomato sauce will be a hit. And, whatever you cook, if you can make it look like a pizza, even better. In fact, if any of the following dinner dishes were delivered to the door in thirty minutes or less, there wouldn't be a bite left in ten minutes. Then there'd be plenty of time to argue over who loads the dishwasher.

THE Á LA KING

Dolly B. Evans
Palos Heights, IL

This is a classic recipe handed down from my mother. It is a favorite of our four children and has been since they were tiny tots. My son named it. When my six young nephews come to visit us from Wisconsin, they always insist that I make THE á la King for them. They always exclaim how great it smells while I'm preparing it. It is tasty, nourishing, fast and easy to prepare.

½ cup green pepper, diced

1 jar (4½ ounces) sliced mushrooms, reserve ¼ cup liquid

½ cup butter

½ cup flour

1 teaspoon salt

¼ teaspoon pepper

1 cup half-and-half

1 cup milk

1¾ cups chicken broth

½ cup frozen peas, cooked

2 to 3 cups chicken, cooked and cubed

1 jar (4 ounces) pimientos, chopped

1 package (6-count) PEPPERIDGE FARM® puff pastry shells

In large skillet, sauté green pepper and mushrooms in butter for 5 minutes. Blend in flour, salt and pepper. Simmer, stirring until mixture is bubbly. Remove from heat. Stir in half-and-half, milk, broth, and reserved mushroom liquid. Heat to boiling. Stirring constantly, boil for 1 minute. Add peas, chicken and pimientos. Cook 4 more minutes. Serve in pastry shells. **Serves 6.**

Serve with mashed potatoes and cranberry sauce.

BAKED CRISPY CHICKEN

Betty Lynn Seidmon, Ph.D.
Daytona Beach, FL

I was seeking low- or no-cholesterol dishes for my family who wants taste without salt and extra sugar. Taste and health do go together. Company likes this dish, too.

KELLOGG'S® NUTRI-GRAIN™ wheat cereal flakes
Whole chicken, cut up and skinned
3 egg whites, slightly beaten
Cooking spray
Seasoning to taste: we use salt-free choices such as SPIKE®, parsley flakes, ground oregano or Italian seasonings

Crush flakes in a sealed plastic bag using a rolling pin (kids like this part). Dip chicken parts, 1 or 2 pieces at a time, in beaten egg whites and drop into plastic bag and shake. Place each flake-covered piece on a cookie sheet which has been lightly sprayed with cooking spray.

Bake in a preheated 400° oven for 20 to 25 minutes, turn pieces over and bake for 10 to 15 additional minutes until crispy on both sides.

Can remain in oven at low temperature covered. After 20 minutes, remove cover and turn off oven. Freezes well, packs for picnics.
Serves 6.

Serve with tomato sauce and pasta.

CHICKEN TAMALE PIE

Mrs. Tignor M. Thompson
Dallas, TX

Either I am the most gullible mother alive, or my kids actually enjoy most everything I cook. Naturally, I choose to believe the latter. Here is a dish they request most often, especially when they're having friends in for dinner. A nice tossed salad and tortilla chips and the meal is complete. Then, you just wait for those smiles.

Tamale Pie:

2 cans (15 ounces) tamales with juice or same amount fresh
1 can CAMPBELL'S® Golden Mushroom soup
1 large onion, chopped
1 can (15 ounces) chili without beans
½ cup rice, uncooked
3 to 4 chicken breasts, skinless, boned and cut into bite-sized pieces
12 ounces white sauce
Cheddar cheese, grated

White Sauce:

4½ tablespoons butter
6 tablespoons flour
½ teaspoon salt
1½ cups milk

Tamale Pie: In large casserole dish layer tamales, soup, onion, chili, rice and chicken. Set aside and prepare the sauce.

White Sauce: Melt butter in saucepan over low heat. Blend in flour, salt (and dash of white pepper if you like). Add milk and cook quickly, stirring constantly until mixture thickens. Remove sauce from heat when it begins to bubble.

Spread white sauce over the top of the pie and sprinkle with cheese. Bake in a 350° oven for 1 hour. Can be assembled a day in advance, covered tightly with plastic wrap and refrigerated. **Serves 6 to 8.**

Serve pie with tortilla chips and salsa.

CHICKEN TETRAZZINI

Teresa D. Rajala, M.D.
Allen, TX

Chicken Tetrazzini is a recipe from my mother's collection. My whole family enjoys this and almost always asks for second helpings.

¼ cup margarine
¼ cup flour
½ teaspoon salt
¼ teaspoon pepper
1 cup chicken broth
1 cup heavy cream
½ package (of 12-ounce package) spaghetti, cooked and drained
2 cups chicken, cooked, cubed and drained
1 can (3 ounces) mushrooms, drained
½ cup Parmesan cheese, grated

Heat oven to 350°. Melt margarine in a large pan. Add flour, salt and pepper. Cook over low heat, stirring until smooth and bubbly. Remove from heat. Stir in broth and cream. Heat to boiling, stirring constantly. Boil and stir for 1 minute. Stir in spaghetti, chicken and mushrooms. Pour into ungreased 2-quart casserole dish. Sprinkle with cheese. Bake uncovered for about 30 minutes or until bubbly. Place under broiler for a few minutes to brown.

Serves 6.

Serve with fruit salad and garlic bread.

CHICKEN ZUCCHINI

Terre Thomas
Beverly Hills, CA

It's my own creation. When my children were young, I wanted to feed them something that looked fun but would still be healthy. It was so tasty that even today my kids ask for it.

Terre Thomas continues to carry on the tradition of her father, the late Danny Thomas, in her support of St. Jude Children's Research Hospital, which he founded.

4 chicken breasts, skinless and fat-free
2 large zucchinis, grated
2 tablespoons lemon juice
Garlic powder or chopped garlic
Margarine, a dab on each breast
Salt

Soak the chicken with lemon juice, cut aluminum foil in pieces large enough to wrap each breast separately. Place 1 breast over the aluminum foil, then sprinkle with garlic powder and salt. Add a little dab of butter. Then place on top enough grated zucchini to cover the whole breast. Then wrap it all in foil. Do the same with each chicken breast. After you have wrapped them all, put them in a baking dish big enough to have each breast two inches apart and cook at 375° for 30 minutes. To serve, unwrap each chicken breast carefully and pour the juice from the foil over it. **Serves 4.**

Great with rice and cooked baby carrots.

GRANDMA'S CHICKEN AND DUMPLINGS

Pamela Morse
Houston, TX

This recipe was handed down to me by my mother, who got it from her mother, Grandma Katie. Although Grandma Katie has been dead for over twenty-five years, I can still remember her wonderful cooking. This recipe was always one of my favorites as a child, and now it is a favorite of both of my children who are eight and twelve and who hardly ever like the same foods.

When the kids' friends come in while the dumplings are cooking: *"Taste Mom's dumplings. You won't believe how good they are!"*

4 chicken breasts, skinned
4 chicken bouillon cubes
1 onion, chopped
2 stalks celery, chopped
Salt and pepper
2 cups flour
1 tablespoon baking powder
1 teaspoon salt
⅛ teaspoon pepper
1 teaspoon poultry seasoning
4 tablespoons cooking oil
1 cup milk

Place chicken, bouillon, onion, celery and seasonings in a large pot with water to cover and boil for 20 minutes or until tender. Remove chicken breasts, bone and shred. Mix together flour, baking powder, salt, pepper and poultry seasoning. Add the oil and milk and blend lightly. Drop by spoonfuls into the simmering broth. Cover and steam 15 minutes. **Serves 8.**

Serve chicken and dumplings with hot biscuits and butter.

LEMON CHICKEN

Janet Stevenson
Kansas City, MO

A dear friend whom I lived with in Dallas before my marriage gave this recipe to me. She and I loved to cook fun food for a few old friends.

"You mean you're making that chicken dish with the sauce, that I love?"

4 boneless, skinless chicken breasts, cut into strips
1 cup flour
1 teaspoon salt
1 teaspoon pepper
¼ cup clarified butter
¾ cup chicken stock
2 tablespoons lemon juice
1 tablespoon parsley, chopped

Flatten chicken between two pieces of waxed paper. Dredge in flour seasoned with salt and pepper. Pour clarified butter into frying pan and lightly brown chicken. Add chicken stock, lemon juice and parsley. Bring to a boil and cook for 8 minutes. **Serves 4.**

CHICKEN AND RICE

Richard D.
Grossnickle, M.D.
Paris, TX

My 5½-year-old daughter Emily always enjoys this recipe when I cook it for her. As I recall, I got it from a girlfriend when I was in college and have served it at many a small dinner party ever since.

4 chicken breasts
½ teaspoon paprika
½ teaspoon garlic salt
½ teaspoon pepper
4 teaspoons butter
1 cup long grain rice
1 can (10½ ounces) chicken with rice soup
1 can (10½ ounces) water

Season each chicken breast with paprika, garlic salt and pepper. Put 1 teaspoon of butter on the top of each breast. Broil for 10 minutes or until skin is browned. Evenly distribute rice over the bottom of a glass dish. Layer chicken over rice. Add soup and 1 can of water. Cover with foil and bake at 350° for 45 minutes. **Serves 4.**

Serve chicken with steamed green beans.

ORIENTAL CHICKEN WINGS

Laurel Sung
Dallas, TX

The use of soy sauce, sugar, sesame oil, green onions, garlic, etc., is standard fare in Chinese kitchens for marinating meat in sundry combinations, usually before stir frying. I think I've found a serendipitous combination for the wings and have found the baking method easier (less messy) than frying.

Because the chicken wings resemble crabs to my children (who are three and five), they call this recipe *"Crab Chicken."*

12 chicken wings, or 4 drumsticks and 4 thighs
½ to ⅓ cup soy sauce
1 tablespoon brown sugar
2 tablespoons water
1 tablespoon sesame oil
2 tablespoons green onions, diced
1 tablespoon garlic, diced
1 tablespoon ginger, diced

Combine all the above ingredients and marinate at least 4 hours. Preheat the oven to 375°. Put chicken wings without juice in deep-dish baking pan, skin side down. Bake for 20 minutes. Turn the chicken wings to skin side up and add the marinating juice. Bake for 15 additional minutes (20 minutes for drumsticks and thighs). Then turn heat to 500° and bake for 5 more minutes to brown the skin. **Serves 8.**

Serve with white rice and steamed asparagus or broccoli.

PINEAPPLE CHICKEN

Saundra Reiter Shapiro
Marietta, GA

This was one of the few ways my daughters, Courtney and Morgan, would eat chicken. It can all be prepared in advance. It is very easy to make and tastes delicious.

Batter:

6 chicken breasts, skinned and boned
2 eggs, beaten
2 tablespoons oil
½ cup water
1 cup flour
½ teaspoon baking powder
¾ teaspoon salt
1 tablespoon paprika
Oil for frying

Sauce:

½ cup ketchup
¼ cup white vinegar
¾ cup cold water
2 tablespoons lemon juice
1¼ cups white sugar
½ cup brown sugar, packed
3 tablespoons cornstarch
¼ cup cold water

Pineapple Chicken:

1 can (15¼ ounces) pineapple chunks, drained well.

Batter: Wash chicken. Cut chicken into 2-inch strips with sharp knife. Beat eggs well. Blend in oil and water, then add remaining dry ingredients. Mix well. Dip chicken strips in batter. Fry in hot oil until golden on all sides. Drain well on paper towel.

Sauce: In a saucepan, combine ketchup, vinegar, water, lemon juice, sugar and brown sugar. Bring to a boil. Simmer for about 2 to 3 minutes. Dissolve cornstarch into ¼ cup cold water. Mix into sauce. Simmer until thickened, stirring occasionally. Cool and store in a tightly closed jar in refrigerator. The sauce can be made in advance. (This sauce is also good with fried fish.)

Pineapple Chicken: Place fried chicken into a glass dish and cover with sauce. Arrange pineapple chunks over chicken. Bake in oven at 350° for about 20 minutes or until sauce is bubbly. **Serves 4 to 6.**

Serve chicken with white rice or Chinese fried rice.

POULET VALLÉE D'AUGE

Danielle Daley Fox
Summit, NJ

This is a family recipe handed down from my grandmother. Children love the chicken in the rich sauce, and it is a great way to get them to eat vegetables.

1 carrot, minced
1 leek, white part only, minced
2 shallots, minced
3 tablespoons butter
1 chicken (3½ pounds) cut into pieces
2½ tablespoons brandy
1 teaspoon salt
1 teaspoon pepper
1 fresh sprig thyme
1 bay leaf
1 can (10½ ounces) chicken broth
5 ounces mushrooms, sliced
3 egg yolks
⅓ cup heavy cream

In a large saucepan, sauté carrot, leek and shallots in 2 tablespoons of butter until tender. Remove and set aside. Sauté the chicken pieces until brown. Add vegetables. Ignite the brandy and sprinkle with salt and pepper. Add the herbs and chicken broth. Cover and simmer over low flame for 30 minutes. In a separate pan, cook mushrooms with remaining butter. Add to chicken. Continue simmering for another 10 minutes. Watch carefully to see if extra liquid is needed. Remove the herbs. Place the pieces of chicken on a serving plate. Cook the sauce for another 5 minutes, uncovered. Remove from the heat and thicken by blending in the egg yolks and cream. Pour over the chicken. **Serves 6.**

Serve with chilled white grape juice.

ROASTED CHICKEN WITH GARLIC AND FRESH HERBS

Diane Kessler
Newport Beach, CA

I've had this recipe for a long time—can't remember where it came from.

6 tablespoons unsalted butter, at room temperature
1½ tablespoons fresh thyme, finely chopped
1½ tablespoons fresh rosemary, finely chopped
1½ tablespoons fresh sage, finely chopped
2 cloves garlic, finely minced
1 whole chicken (3½ pounds)
½ teaspoon salt
¼ teaspoon black pepper, freshly ground

Combine butter, thyme, rosemary, sage and garlic in a small bowl. Mash mixture with fork to form a paste. Remove any excess fat from chicken's tail and neck cavities. Loosen skin by carefully running fingers between skin and meat along breast, legs and thighs. Divide butter and herb paste into four parts. Stuff one part into each leg and breast. Press skin with fingers to distribute paste evenly. Season outside of chicken to taste with salt and pepper. Place in roasting pan and roast at 425° for 20 minutes on each side and 20 minutes breast side up. Set aside to cool for 15 minutes before slicing.
Serves 4.

Serve chicken with twice-baked potatoes and steamed carrots.

STEVE'S CHICKEN PAPRIKASH

Joy Ciko
Huntington Harbour, CA

This secret recipe was shared with me by my Hungarian-born husband who prepares it from memory the way his mother made it. Throughout our thirty-six years of marriage it has been a favorite with many guests of ours and of our daughter's, too.

Chicken:

1 large fryer, cut into pieces
2 tablespoons oil
2 large white onions, sliced
1 tablespoon paprika
Salt and pepper
1 pint sour cream
1 recipe soft noodles

Soft Noodles:

½ cup milk
1 egg, beaten
1 teaspoon salt
2 cups flour
3 quarts boiling water

Chicken: Brown the chicken in hot oil. Remove chicken and then sauté onions in the same pan. Return chicken to pan and add paprika, salt and pepper. Cover and simmer on low heat for 30 to 40 minutes until chicken is tender. Remove and keep warm while preparing sauce and noodles. Into pan juices, carefully stir sour cream. Stir until hot and pour over chicken, reserving some of the sauce to pass in a dish.

Soft Noodles: Stir milk, egg, flour and salt to make a fairly stiff dough. Spread out a spoonful of dough on a wet board. Cut into small strips (¼x1-inch long). Drop into hot boiling water. When the noodles are cooked they will rise to the top of the pan. Remove with slotted spoon. Place chicken on a hot serving platter with the soft noodles. Serve at once. (Cook's note: This recipe may be served with packaged noodles.) **Serves 8 to 10.**

Serve chicken with fresh steamed vegetables.

STEWED CHICKEN

Bettye Fisher
Inglewood, CA

Given to me by my adopted mother to be carried on through the generations.

One whole chicken, cut into parts
½ teaspoon salt
1 teaspoon black pepper
2 green onions, chopped
2 garlic cloves, chopped
½ cup lemon juice
1 tablespoon vinegar
1 tablespoon oregano
1 tablespoon thyme
1 yellow onion, chopped
1 teaspoon soy sauce
¼ cup rum (optional)
1½ tablespoons sugar
2 tablespoons canola oil
¼ cup Italian seasonings

In a large plastic bag combine chicken, salt, pepper, green onions, cloves, lemon juice, vinegar, oregano, thyme, yellow onion, soy sauce and rum and close the bag. Allow the mixture to marinate overnight.

Brown the sugar with the oil. Add the chicken and brown. Pour the liquid mixture from the bag over the chicken. Add water if needed to cover the chicken halfway. Cover and cook over low heat for 45 minutes. **Serves 6 to 8.**

Serve chicken with Rice Alfredo on page 127, and a crisp green salad.

MOM'S SPICY CHICKEN PASTA

Roxanne Rivera
Tijeras, NM

My kids love pasta. I am always trying to add a southwestern flair to anything I cook. This is easy and tasty enough for the kids and good enough to serve to company.

My little eight-year-old insists that someday I will put avocado in her CHEERIOS® cereal.

1 pound boneless, skinless chicken breasts, cubed
1 small red onion, chopped
2 tablespoons olive oil
1 large tomato, chopped
1 can (7 ounces) green chilies, chopped
1 package (16 ounces) pasta, cooked
1 pint whipping cream
1 large avocado, chopped

In a medium-sized skillet combine chicken, red onion and olive oil. Cook approximately 5 minutes or until tender. Season to taste. Add tomato and green chilies. Cook for 3 minutes. Add chicken mixture to pasta. Slowly stir in whipping cream and avocado. Serve immediately. **Serves 4.**

Note: Two teaspoons of garlic will make an excellent addition.

You can prepare pasta without chicken and serve as a side dish.

MERMAID DINNER

Deborah Bartelstein
Glencoe, IL

I was inspired by the movie, *"The Little Mermaid"*. My 6½-, 4-, and 2½-year-olds go crazy for this nutritious meal and I made it up so they would eat a healthy (non-chemical) meal happily.

"I don't even have room for dessert."

1 tablespoon butter

1½ pounds extra lean ground turkey

Salt to taste

Garlic powder to taste

1 to 1½ pounds spinach, cleaned and steamed

2 tablespoons butter, melted

½ teaspoon salt

1 package (16 ounces) large pasta shells

1 jar (16 ounces) natural spaghetti sauce

1½ cups Mozzarella cheese, grated

Spray skillet with nonstick cooking spray, add butter and melt over medium-high heat. Add ground turkey. Sprinkle with salt and garlic powder to taste. Cook until well done. Drain steamed spinach and toss with butter and salt to taste. Cook pasta shells according to package directions. Drain and run under cold water. When cool, fill pasta shells with cooked turkey. Place spinach on individual, microwavable plates so a bed of spinach is created. This is our seaweed base! Place 3 filled pasta shells on each plate. Spoon spaghetti sauce on top of shells only. Sprinkle desired amount of cheese on top of sauce and pasta shells only. Microwave till cheese is just melted. **Serves 6 to 8.**

Serve with cheese toast and crisp green salad.

MOM'S SUPER SNEAKY SALAD

Susan
(Mrs. William Terry) Barbee
Weslaco, TX

I came up with this salad one evening when my family wanted Italian, but I was tired of the same old spaghetti and lasagna. They had all cleaned their plates long before they realized they'd each consumed a *"Mom-friendly"* amount of spinach!

"It's so good you don't even know it's good for you!"
Tracy Barbee (age 7).

1 package (16 ounces) shaped pasta
1 pound ground turkey
2 cloves garlic, crushed
1 teaspoon dried basil
1 teaspoon paprika
1½ teaspoons sugar
1 teaspoon black pepper, freshly ground
1½ teaspoons onion powder
1 teaspoon salt
1 package (10 ounces) frozen spinach, thawed
1 small pinch nutmeg
1 bottle (8 ounces) ranch dressing
¾ cup Parmesan, freshly grated

Cook pasta according to package directions. Drain and set aside.

In a medium skillet, brown turkey and garlic. Add remaining seasonings, except nutmeg. Drain the spinach and add it and the nutmeg, tossing until well mixed. Cook until spinach is sufficiently heated, about 10 to 12 minutes. Remove from heat.

Place pasta in a large salad bowl. Add the turkey-spinach mixture. Pour the salad dressing over mixture and sprinkle with Parmesan cheese. Toss until all of the ingredients are well coated. **Serves 4 to 6.**

Serve salad with bread sticks and garlic butter.

O'BOY POT ROAST

Mrs. Ileen Tabankin
Naperville, IL

This was my mother's basic recipe to which I added carrots. She did not approve and subsequently disowned my version.

A neighbor's child who is a poor eater and hates most everything asked her mom, *"Why can't you make pot roast like Mrs. Tabankin?"*

3 to 4 pounds lean brisket
10 cups tomato sauce
1 teaspoon salt
1 teaspoon pepper
1 teaspoon paprika
1 teaspoon garlic powder
1 teaspoon onion powder
8 large potatoes, peeled and cut in half
1 pound carrots, peeled and cut in half
5 medium-sized onions peeled and quartered
5 cloves garlic, minced

Wash brisket and place in 6-quart pot with a little water underneath. Add tomato sauce and spices to taste. Cover pot and cook on medium flame for 15 to 20 minutes. Remove brisket and transfer to cutting board or platter. With a sharp knife, slice against the grain, lengthwise. Return to the pot and add vegetables. Cover. After 10 minutes, adjust heat to medium-low temperature. Check periodically and rearrange meat and vegetables to prevent burning. Cook thoroughly, approximately 1½ hours. **Serves 8 to 10.**

Serve with steamed green beans and biscuits.

MOM'S FRIDAY BRISKET

Beth M. Brown
Dallas, TX

My mom always made this brisket on Fridays and it always tasted good, even several days later. The meat is very tender. You don't even need to add ketchup.

3 large onions, sliced
1 large brisket
Fresh garlic
⅓ cup brown sugar
⅓ cup chili sauce
1 can (12 ounces) beer

Preheat oven to 350°. Slice onions and place on the bottom of a roasting pan. Place brisket on top of the onions. On top of brisket crush fresh garlic, covering most of top of brisket. Combine brown sugar, chili sauce and beer. Pour over the brisket while beer is still foaming. Cover tightly and put in 350° oven for 4 hours. If you like the top of your brisket brown, uncover 20 minutes before removing from oven. Remember to cut brisket against the grain. **Serves 10 to 12.**

Serve brisket with potatoes sliced in round pieces and added to the roaster 1½ hours before removing brisket from oven.

SODA POP BRISKET

Arlene Blut
Las Vegas, NV

My children always wanted this when they were young. This recipe is so easy I make it in the morning before leaving for work. The oven goes on at noon and when I come home about 3:00 p.m. I uncover it and add the potatoes. It is delicious by 6:00 p.m. for dinner. Wonderful cold the next day for sandwiches. The soda pop makes the best gravy in the world.

1 package dry onion soup mix
1 teaspoon paprika
1 teaspoon garlic powder
1 large brisket
1 can DIET PEPSI®
3 medium potatoes, quartered

Sprinkle soup mix, paprika and garlic powder on both sides of a large brisket. Place in an oven roaster. Pour soda over seasoned brisket. Bake at 250° for 2 to 3 hours, depending upon size of brisket. Uncover, add potatoes and more soda if needed. Turn oven to 300° and roast until potatoes are brown and meat is tender, about another 1 to 1½ hours. **Serves 6 to 8.**

DAD'S SPECIAL STEAK BAKE

Karen Green
Irvine, CA

Occasionally Dad puts on the apron and cooks a special Sunday night dinner. For meat lovers—like our kids—this recipe is sensational.

Special Sauce:

¼ cup butter
¾ pound mushrooms, thinly sliced
1 medium onion, chopped
½ teaspoon garlic powder
Salt and pepper to taste
3 cans (15 ounces each) tomato sauce
1 teaspoon sugar
½ teaspoon oregano
½ cup dry red wine

Steak:

1 (3 pounds) thick sirloin steak
1 pound Monterey Jack cheese, shredded

For the sauce: Melt butter and sauté mushrooms, onion and garlic until vegetables are light brown. Season with salt and pepper. Add tomato sauce, sugar, oregano and red wine. Simmer for 30 minutes.

Broil the steak until very rare. Cut into 2-inch cubes. Place in casserole and pour on sauce just to cover. Top with shredded cheese. Bake in preheated 400° oven for 10 minutes.

Slide under broiler to brown cheese. **Serves 8.**

Serve with crisp green salad and baked potatoes.

BEEF MEATBALLS STROGANOFF

Kae Walters
Cincinnati, OH

Good as an appetizer or main dish.

1 pound lean ground beef
1 teaspoon salt
Dash ground red pepper
½ teaspoon ground cumin seed
¾ teaspoon ground coriander seed
⅓ cup bread crumbs, finely ground
1 tablespoon olive oil
2 cups onion, sliced
2 cups mushrooms, sliced
1 teaspoon lemon juice
1 beef bouillon cube
Salt and pepper
Garlic salt
1 cup sour cream
1 tablespoon paprika

Combine ground beef, salt, red pepper, cumin, coriander and bread crumbs. Shape into small balls and brown in olive oil. Add the onions and sauté until limp. Add mushrooms, lemon juice, bouillon cube and seasonings. Sauté until mushrooms are tender. Top with sour cream and paprika. Heat thoroughly and serve.
Serves 4 to 6.

Serve stroganoff with steamed white rice and asparagus.

CHILI MEAT

Sandra Matteucci
Phoenix, AZ

The kids are grown now. However, as young children, one (the boy) always said *"wow"* when this was served. The other child (the girl) always said *"yuk."* So take a taste and decide for yourself. I still love it.

1½ pounds round steak, ¼-inch thick
4 tablespoons soy sauce
¼ cup flour
4 tablespoons oil
1 can (7 ounces) diced green chilies
1 cup water

Cut steak into bite-sized pieces. Brush soy sauce on each side of meat. Sprinkle with flour. Brown steak in oil. Add chilies and water. Cover and simmer until meat is tender. **Serves 6.**

You may include pinto beans and rice with the Chili Meat.

DOUBLE EASY STEW

Mary "Dee" Faxel
Fort Worth, TX

When our family returned from a long vacation late in the day, I looked in the freezer and the pantry, defrosted the stew meat and raided the pantry. This was the result.

#1 child asked for another helping. #2 child said, *"Let's have this again tomorrow!"* #3 child said, *"And again the next day!"* #4 child remarked, *"Gosh, this is almost as good as Grandma's!"*

1½ cups flour
1 teaspoon pepper
2 pounds lean stew meat cut into 1-inch cubes
1 can (14½ ounces) chicken broth
1 can (14½ ounces) beef broth
1 can (11½ ounces) tomato juice
2 tablespoons Worcestershire sauce
2 tablespoons A-1® steak sauce
1 can (8 ounces) onions, drained
1 can (16 ounces) corn, drained
1 can (16 ounces) carrots, drained
1 can (8 ounces) mushrooms, drained
1 can (14½ ounces) tomatoes, chopped, not drained
2 packages beef gravy
2 tablespoons water

Flour and pepper stew meat. Place in a large kettle. Add chicken and beef broths and tomato juice. Add the sauces. Simmer for 30 to 35 minutes, covered. Add all other ingredients and cook over low heat for 20 minutes. Thicken with packaged gravy which has been softened with water. Increase heat and stir until stew thickens, 3 to 4 minutes. **Serves 12.**

Serve stew with hot corn bread muffins.

FRIEND'S MEAT LOAF

Ann (Mrs. Craig)
McDonald
Ralls, TX

This meat loaf recipe was given to me by a friend thirty-three years ago. It is one of the most delicious and successful dishes I prepare. I often fix it in larger quantities for family gatherings.

"Mom, puh-leeze make meat loaf tonight!"

Meat Loaf:

1½ pounds ground beef or ground turkey
1 egg
1 slice bread, torn into pieces
Seasonings to taste
1 tablespoon dried minced onion
Dash garlic powder
½ can (of 8-ounce can) tomato sauce

Sauce:

3 tablespoons brown sugar
2 tablespoons prepared mustard
2 tablespoons Worcestershire sauce
3 tablespoons cider vinegar
1 can (8 ounces) tomato sauce

Preheat oven to 350°. Mix all meat loaf ingredients well and form into a loaf. Place in a shallow baking pan. Combine all ingredients for sauce and pour over loaf. Bake uncovered for 1½ hours. **Serves 6.**

Serve meat loaf with twice-baked potatoes and green beans.

MEAT PIN WHEELS

Ruth Ann Renick
Rolla, MO

I've had this recipe in my file probably since 1964. It became a favorite of my husband and children.

This was our twenty-nine-year-old daughter's favorite childhood meal. She said that *"the pinwheels were great cause for excitement when I came home from school and saw them for dinner."*

1 pound ground beef
1 cup packaged prepared biscuit mix
½ cup milk
2 tablespoons butter, melted
3 tablespoons ketchup
2 teaspoons prepared mustard
1 teaspoon instant minced onion

In a medium skillet, brown ground beef and drain. Heat oven to 450°. In a small bowl mix biscuit mix and milk together to form a soft dough. Roll out dough into a 12-inch square on a floured board or floured waxed paper. Mix together butter, ketchup, mustard and onion. Spread evenly over dough. Crumble ground beef evenly over dough. Roll up jelly roll fashion and cut into 8 slices. Place slices, cut side up, on a lightly greased baking sheet and bake at 350° for 12 to 15 minutes or until biscuits are golden brown. **Serves 4.**

NOTE: When we prepare these pin wheels today, we use the reduced-fat ground beef or ground turkey. It is easier to use waxed paper when rolling out and rolling up the dough.

Serve with fresh mushroom sauce.

WORKING MOM'S EASY POT PIE

Mrs. C.W. Schoenvogel
College Station, TX

Kids love this and it's as easy as 1-2-3. This recipe, which has been used in our family by everyone, was given to me by a busy, working mom. There are never any leftovers.

1 (9-inch) pie shell
1 pound ground beef
1 medium onion, chopped
1 package (10 ounces) frozen mixed vegetables, thawed
1 can cream of chicken soup
Salt and pepper to taste

Sauté ground beef with onion. Remove grease. Drain vegetables and add to meat. Add soup. Stir to combine. Pour into prepared pie shell. Bake at 350° for 25 to 30 minutes. **Serves 6.**

7-LAYER CASSEROLE

Elizabeth Bernsen
Chevy Chase, MD

This casserole is so good I've even served it for dinner parties. Sometimes I think it's even better reheated.

1 cup uncooked rice
1 cup canned whole kernel corn, drained
1 teaspoon salt
1 teaspoon pepper
2 cans (8 ounces each) tomato sauce
½ cup water
½ cup onion, chopped
½ cup green pepper, chopped
½ cup celery, chopped
¾ pound ground beef, uncooked
¼ cup water
4 strips bacon, halved

Preheat oven to 350°. Layer the following in a 2-quart baking dish with a tight-fitting lid: rice, corn, salt, pepper, 1 can of tomato sauce, water, onion, green pepper, celery and ground beef. Pour the second can of tomato sauce and remaining water over layered ingredients. Lay 4 strips of bacon on top. Cover and bake for 1 hour. Uncover and bake for 15 to 30 minutes, until bacon is crisp. **Serves 6 to 8.**

Serve casserole with tossed green salad.

OLD COUNTRY SHEPHERD'S PIE

Heather Stern
Chicago, IL

This old Scottish recipe was a weekly feature in my childhood and has become as big a hit with my three children and our many dinner guests.

1½ pounds ground beef
½ pound carrots, peeled and cubed
1 large onion, peeled and chopped
1 bouillon cube
1 cup boiling water
Pepper, thyme, basil and marjoram to taste
1 can (16 ounces) corn, drained
1 can (16 ounces) peas, drained
8 medium potatoes, boiled and mashed
1 teaspoon salt

Brown beef quickly in large skillet. Add carrots and onion, mixing well. Pour in bouillon cube which has been dissolved in boiling water. Add preferred spices and simmer for 1 hour or until beef is fully cooked and vegetables tender but not mushy. Add vegetables. Mix well and spoon mixture into the bottom of a 10-inch glass pie plate. Combine potatoes and salt and spread on top of the meat mixture and whip up lightly with fork or score in lines. Bake in 350° oven for 30 minutes or until top is lightly browned. **Serves 8.**

Serve with a side salad or homemade cole slaw.

GERMAN GOULASH

Dorothea M. Park
Warren, PA

This recipe comes from my mother in Germany. Every time I cook it, the marvelous aroma still brings back fond memories.

Children love it because the meat is so tender and easy to eat. They say, *"It's awesome!"*

1 pound sirloin tip, cubed
1 pound pork, cubed
Salt and pepper to taste
2 onions, sliced
3 cups water
1 cup dry red wine
2 chicken bouillon cubes
½ teaspoon garlic powder
2 tablespoons ketchup, optional
2 tablespoons cornstarch
½ cup water

In a large pot, brown one layer of sirloin tip and pork at a time. Remove each layer after browning. Season each layer with salt and pepper to taste. With the last layer, brown onions. Return all browned meat to pot and add water, wine, bouillon cubes and garlic powder. Add ketchup, if desired. Simmer for 1½ hours, or until meat is tender. Make a paste with cornstarch and water. Add gradually to boiling goulash to thicken broth. **Serves 6 to 8.**

Serve goulash over rice or noodles.

SANTA FE SURPRISE

Catherine Walker
Los Gatos, CA

This was truly created by surprise. One Thursday night, without enough time to get to the market, we threw together anything that sounded Mexican and, voila!

"When I grow up and have a man-friend, I'm going to make this every night." Miss Morgan Walker (age 4).

1 pound ground beef
1 onion, chopped
½ green bell pepper, chopped
3 tablespoon chili powder or packaged chili mix
1 cup tomato sauce
2 eggs, beaten
1 cup light cream
1 package (16 ounces) corn chips
⅓ cup Jack cheese, grated
⅔ cup sour cream
¾ cup Cheddar cheese, grated

In a medium saucepan, combine beef, onion, green pepper, chili powder and tomato sauce. Simmer 5 minutes. Add eggs and light cream slowly. In a 1-quart casserole, place corn chips in bottom. Top with one-half of the meat mixture, then Jack cheese. Repeat layering. Top with sour cream and Cheddar cheese. Bake at 325° for 25 to 30 minutes. **Serves 6 to 8.**

Serve dish with green salad and orange slices.

PAPRIKASH

Joan Lunden
New York, NY

This is a recipe that I got from my mother-in-law, Joie Krauss. She always made it for her kids when they were growing up. I happen to love it, and I have made it part of my repertoire.

1 medium onion, diced
2 tablespoons butter
1 green pepper, seeded and sliced
Salt, pepper and paprika, to taste
2 or 3 potatoes, diced
1 can (16 ounces) whole tomatoes, chopped, reserving juice
Water
6 to 8 hot dogs, sliced

Simmer onion in butter. Add green pepper, salt, pepper and paprika. Add potatoes. Mix in tomatoes and the canned tomato juice. Add enough water to cover. Simmer 30 minutes or until potatoes are tender. Add hot dogs. Cook another 8 minutes. **Serves 6.**

GALLEY-HO SKILLET DINNER

Lois Jean
MacFarlane
Kiawah Island, SC

This recipe started with weekend trips on our boat. I could make it in my electric skillet at home and just reheat it after we arrived at the boat.

2 tablespoons butter
1 pound lean ground beef
¾ cup onion, chopped
½ cup celery, chopped
¼ cup green pepper, chopped
1 can (1 pound 12 ounces) tomatoes
1 teaspoon salt
¼ teaspoon pepper
1 cup elbow macaroni or noodles, uncooked
½ cup Parmesan cheese, grated
¾ cup Cheddar cheese, grated
Parsley, chopped

Melt butter in large skillet with cover. Add beef, onion, celery and green pepper and sauté. Add tomatoes, salt, pepper and bring to a boil. Add macaroni. Cover and cook over low heat, stirring occasionally, for about 10 minutes or until tender. Add Parmesan cheese. Stir. Sprinkle with Cheddar cheese. Cover and allow to stand for 5 minutes. Add parsley and serve.
Serves 4 to 6.

MARINATED FLANK STEAK

Elaine Montgomery
Garland, TX

I found this recipe about ten years ago in a community cookbook. It had been submitted by a good friend. I revised it for my family. Everyone who eats it wants the recipe and it then becomes their family's favorite. My teenagers will always be home on time when they know we're having marinated flank steak.

"Best steak in the world."

2 pounds flank steak
¾ cup vegetable oil
¼ cup soy sauce
¼ cup honey
2 tablespoons white vinegar
2 tablespoons onion, chopped
¼ teaspoon garlic powder
¼ teaspoon ginger

Cut partially frozen steak into 1-inch strips. In a shallow dish combine oil, soy sauce, honey, vinegar, onion, garlic powder and ginger. Place steak in marinade, cover and chill overnight. Grill over hot coals 10 minutes on each side or until sufficiently cooked, basting often with the marinade. **Serves 4.**

MUSHROOM AND ONION SAUCE

Chris Larson
Fort Worth, TX

I always asked my mother to make this when I returned home from school. It is rich, but a serving is only meant to be two spoonfuls.

2 large yellow onions, sliced
1 tablespoon oil
1 tablespoon water
1 can (8 ounces) mushrooms, sliced
1 carton (8 ounces) sour cream
2 tablespoons fresh dill, chopped

In a large nonstick skillet, brown onions in oil, then add water, cover and simmer for 5 minutes. Add mushrooms, simmering until vegetables are soft and water absorbed. Add sour cream and dill. Lower heat and stir. **Serves 12.**

Serve sauce as a warm condiment to any meat. You can add cooked ground beef and serve it over rice.

GREEN ENCHILADAS

Darla Bennett
Sulphur Springs, TX

My three daughters are grown now but when they were all at home this recipe was on the top of their list.

"When can we have Mama Eddie's enchiladas? We love them the most!"

1 pound ground chuck
1 teaspoon salt
1 teaspoon pepper
1 jar (12 ounces) chunky picante sauce
1 can cream of mushroom soup
1 can (4 ounces) green chilies, chopped
1 carton (8 ounces) sour cream
8 to 10 large flour tortillas
1 pound Cheddar cheese, grated

Brown ground chuck with salt and pepper to taste. Add chunky picante sauce. Set aside.

Mix cream of mushroom soup, green chilies and sour cream. Heat but do not boil. Fill the center of tortillas with the meat mixture. Roll each one up and place close together in an oblong pan. Pour the liquid mixture over the filled tortillas. Top with Cheddar cheese. Heat in a 350° oven until cheese melts. **Serves 6 to 8.**

Serve enchiladas with refried beans and rice.

MEXICAN FIESTA CASSEROLE

Mrs. Jimmy J. Jones
Houston, TX

I have four sons and this has been one of their most requested repeat performance dishes. My recipe card for this has *"men love"* in the top corner.

"I don't like anything else on the table but THAT." (the casserole)

1 pound ground meat
½ cup onion, chopped
1 clove garlic
1 can (16 ounces) stewed tomatoes
1 package (8 ounces) taco sauce
1 can (4 ounces) green chilies, chopped
4 beef bouillon cubes
⅓ cup water
2 tablespoons flour
1½ cups cheese, shredded
1 cup biscuit baking mix
¾ cup milk
3 eggs
2 tablespoons yellow cornmeal

Preheat oven to 375°. In large skillet, brown beef, onion and garlic. Stir in tomatoes, taco sauce, chilies and bouillon. Stir and cook until bouillon dissolves. Stir together water and flour, add to beef and cook until thickened. Put in 3-quart baking dish. Top with half the cheese. In small bowl, beat together biscuit mix, milk and eggs. Pour over casserole. Top with remaining cheese and cornmeal. Bake 30 minutes or until a knife inserted in center comes out clean. Let stand 5 minutes before serving. **Serves 8 to 10.**

Serve casserole with refried beans.

SOUTH OF THE BORDER LASAGNA

Nancy Harrell
Houston, TX

I find the best recipes are exchanged through good friends. This one came to me that way. This is the special dish I serve at the bay, not only because it's so fast and easy to prepare, but because it can be prepared ahead of time and can be doubled to serve a large family and friends.

2 pounds ground chuck
1 onion, chopped
1 clove garlic, minced
2 tablespoons chili powder
3 cups tomato sauce
1 teaspoon sugar
1 tablespoon salt
½ cup sliced black olives
1 can (4 ounces) chopped green chilies
12 corn tortillas
Vegetable oil
2 cups small curd cottage cheese
1 egg, beaten
1 cup Monterey Jack cheese, grated
1 cup Cheddar cheese, grated

Topping:
½ cup green onion, chopped
½ cup sour cream
½ cup sliced black olives

Brown meat. Drain. Add onion and garlic and cook until soft. Sprinkle chili powder over meat and mix well. Add tomato sauce, sugar, salt, black olives and chilies. Simmer 15 minutes. While mixture simmers, soften tortillas in hot oil. Drain on paper towels. Beat together cottage cheese and egg. Set aside.

In a 9x13-inch casserole, place one-third of the meat mixture, followed by half of the Monterey Jack cheese, half of the cottage cheese and half of the tortillas. Repeat process, ending with meat sauce on top. Cover with cheese. Bake at 350° for 30 minutes.

Top individual servings with green onion, sour cream and olives. **Serves 8 to 10.**

Serve with chips and salsa.

ROUGH CREEK RANCH CASSEROLE

Mrs. vanAlen Hollomon
Dallas, TX

This was cooked at the ranch for many years by our cook, Louise McCoy. The kids loved it because it was pasta that tasted like a pizza. Boys used to have their mothers call and ask for the recipe. My daughter now cooks it for friends at college.

1 cup onion, chopped
1 pound Italian sausage
1 jar (15 ounces) spaghetti sauce
1 package (12 ounces) rigatoni
4 slices Mozzarella
⅓ cup Parmesan cheese, grated
Pepperoni sausage, sliced

In a medium saucepan, brown onions and sausage. Drain. Pour spaghetti sauce over sausage mixture. Cook rigatoni according to package directions and drain. Place in a large casserole dish. Pour sauce over cooked rigatoni. Top with cheeses. Heat in 350° oven for 10 minutes. Top with sliced pepperoni sausage. Cook 5 more minutes. Can be frozen. Reheat from frozen at 325° for 35 to 40 minutes. **Serves 4 to 6.**

Serve casserole with Italian bread sticks.

DADDY'S EASY PARMIGIANA

Mrs. W. Waller Caldwell, Jr.
McKinney, TX

We all love veal parmigiana but veal is rather expensive. Daddy came up with his version using a pork tenderloin. It's easy and delicious. The kids loved it all their growing-up years.

"Fantastic!"

1 pork tenderloin, butterflied and pounded thin
⅓ cup flour
½ teaspoon garlic salt
½ teaspoon seasoned salt or Greek seasoning
3 tablespoons olive oil
3 cups bottled Marinara sauce
2 cups Mozzarella cheese, shredded
¾ cup Parmesan cheese, shredded

Preheat oven to 350°. Spray a 2-quart baking dish with nonstick coating. Dredge pork in mixture of flour, garlic salt and seasoned salt. Sauté in olive oil until browned on both sides. Remove from heat and drain.

Cover bottom of prepared pan with 1½ cups bottled Marinara sauce. Sprinkle 1 cup Mozzarella over sauce. Place sautéed pork on cheese. Sprinkle ½ cup Parmesan over pork. Pour the remaining 1½ cups Marinara sauce over all. Sprinkle top with remaining 1 cup Mozzarella and ¼ cup Parmesan.

Cover with foil and bake 30 to 40 minutes, until cheese is melted and bubbly. Uncover and place under broiler to brown slightly. Remove from oven and let stand 10 minutes before serving. **Serves 4.**

Serve with pasta of your choice, salad and garlic bread.

UPSIDE-DOWN PIZZA

Cheryl Behan
St. Louis, MO

I make this for dinner when I have a family of out-of-town guests and serve a salad and garlic bread to complete the meal.

This is my answer to *"What's for dinner?"*

1 pound bulk Italian sausage
½ cup onion, chopped
1¼ cups spaghetti or pizza sauce
¼ pound mushrooms, sliced
1 can (2¼ ounces) sliced ripe olives
6 ounces Mozzarella cheese, sliced
2 eggs
1 cup milk
1 tablespoon vegetable oil
1 cup flour
¼ teaspoon salt
⅓ cup Parmesan cheese, grated

Preheat oven to 400°. Fry sausage in 12-inch skillet over medium heat. Add onion and cook, stirring frequently, until onion is limp and sausage is well browned. Drain fat.

Add spaghetti sauce, mushrooms and olives; heat until bubbly. Pour into 9x13x2-inch baking dish. Arrange Mozzarella cheese over sausage mixture.

In blender container, combine eggs, milk, oil, flour and salt. Mix until smooth. Pour evenly over Mozzarella cheese and sprinkle with Parmesan cheese.

Bake uncovered in 400° oven for about 25 minutes or until crust is puffed and golden. Cut into 10 squares and serve hot. **Serves 10.**

Serve pizza with green salad and garlic bread.

SAUSAGE CASSEROLE

Evelyn M. Gunnels
Houston, TX

My daughter-in-law substituted sweetened condensed milk for the evaporated milk one time, causing my daughter to rename this *"The Casserole from Hell."*

2 pounds bulk hot sausage
1 large onion, chopped
1 package (8 ounces) wide noodles
1 can cream of mushroom or celery soup
1 can Cheddar cheese soup
1 can (12 ounces) evaporated milk
1 cup sharp Cheddar cheese, grated
3 tablespoons butter, melted
1 cup Italian-seasoned bread crumbs

In a large skillet, brown sausage and onion. Drain excess fat. Cook noodles according to package directions. Drain and reserve ½ cup of the water. Add soup, milk and reserved water to noodles. Stir in sausage, onion and cheese. Place in a greased 2-quart casserole. Combine butter and bread crumbs and sprinkle over top of mixture. Bake in a 350° oven for 15 to 20 minutes or until brown and bubbly. **Serves 6 to 8.**

Serve casserole with crisp greens.

GRANDMA'S SPAGHETTI

Mrs. Inez Cohen
Winnetka, IL

Our three children are now grown with children of their own, but I remember helping my mother make a nonspicy spaghetti. Now we are on our third generation and it is loved by young and old. Easy and fun to make and easy to digest. When our son was in his rapid-growing years he requested I make extra so there would be leftovers. He loves it cold for breakfast.

½ cup onion, chopped
½ cup green pepper, chopped
1 tablespoon butter
1 pound ground beef
1 can (14½ ounces) tomatoes
1 can (8 ounces) tomato sauce
1 teaspoon Worcestershire sauce
Salt to taste
1 package (12 ounces) spaghetti, cooked
6 slices American cheese

In a medium saucepan, combine onions, green pepper and butter. Add beef and cook about 10 minutes. Add tomatoes, tomato sauce, Worcestershire sauce and salt. Simmer about 1 hour. Cook spaghetti according to package directions. Add tomato mixture to spaghetti and place in 15-inch glass baking dish. Cover with slices of American cheese. Bake in 350° oven for 15 to 20 minutes. **Serves 4.**

The spaghetti is great with tossed salad and garlic bread.

PASTA CARBONARA

Donivee Nash
Arcadia, CA

This recipe evolved as a result of my fondness for cooking and the necessity to take my turn as a volunteer in my children's classes in elementary school. Fifteen years ago when pasta machines were new and trendy (and hand-operated, of course), I would take the ingredients for fresh pasta and the machine into the classroom and the children would all participate in rolling and cutting the dough.

1 pound fusilli or other pasta
1½ sticks butter, melted
3 large cloves garlic, minced
3 eggs, beaten
1 pound bacon, cooked until crisp, drained and crumbled
1½ cups fresh parsley, chopped
¼ pound Parmesan cheese, freshly grated

Cook pasta in boiling water until slightly firm, drain. Sauté butter and garlic and add to the pasta. Add the beaten eggs and stir. Toss in the bacon, parsley and cheese. **Serves 4.**

The ingredients for the sauce are variable in their quantities, subject to individual taste and dietary restrictions. Margarine can be used in place of butter, and the quantities of egg and bacon can be reduced. The raw beaten eggs, when tossed with hot pasta, cook lightly and require no further stove-top cooking.

You can add cooked, chopped chicken or turkey to pasta.

LAMB CHOPS WITH SPICY MINT SAUCE

Ruth Reva Michaelson
Aurora, CO

This is a case of role reversal in that my daughter came up with the recipe after a number of tries. You see, I love lamb, but she's not very fond of it. So, this is our compromise.

"It's the only lamb recipe acceptable to my taste."
Bonny Lee Michaelson, (thirty-something).

4 (6 ounces each) lamb chops
4 teaspoons Worcestershire sauce
Garlic powder to taste
Onion powder to taste
½ cup mint jelly
¼ cup green pepper jelly

Remove excess fat from lamb chops and wash thoroughly. Make small cuts in chops to tenderize. Place chops in nonstick frying pan which has been sprayed with cooking spray. Cook chops on medium heat. Put 3 to 4 drops of Worcestershire sauce on each chop. Sprinkle with garlic and onion powders, then add mint and pepper jellies. Turn chops and repeat on other side. Cover pan and let steam for 15 minutes on medium-high heat. Turn chops over, cook for 10 more minutes. If pan dries, add more jellies. **Serves 4.**

Serve chops with steamed carrots and cauliflower.

HAWAIIAN PORK CHOPS

Joan Chognard
Menlo Park, CA

My oldest child always requested this recipe for his birthday dinner.

"It smells just like I remembered it—good!"

4 pork chops
1 tablespoon brown sugar
4 thin slices of lime
½ cup ketchup
½ cup water

Trim pork chops. Place on greased baking dish. Sprinkle each chop with brown sugar. Place a thin slice of lime on each chop. Mix together ketchup and water and pour over pork chops. Bake at 325° for 1 hour. **Serves 4.**

Serve pork chops with steamed rice and broccoli.

JUICY HAM

Mrs. Henry S. Grant
San Francisco, CA

This is actually my husband's recipe. Over his forty years in the bar business, he has always enjoyed experimenting with spirits in cooking. In this case the alcohol content evaporates, leaving you with a very sweet, juicy ham that kids will love.

10 pound ham
1 cup Blackberry brandy
1 cup orange juice
1 tablespoon vinegar
1 tablespoon lemon juice
2 cups cherry juice

Place ham in a large glass dish. In a separate bowl, combine blackberry brandy, orange juice, vinegar, lemon juice and cherry juice. Pour marinade over the ham. Marinate ham overnight in refrigerator. Bake in a 325° oven, 18 minutes per pound. **Serves 10 to 12.**

Serve ham with white beans and wheat rolls.

COCONUT-BEER SHRIMP

Wendy H. Blanks
Plano, TX

Tradition—this is a light, delicious appetizer for any special dinner, but we serve it every Christmas Eve.

1 teaspoon cayenne pepper
1 teaspoon salt
1 teaspoon black pepper
½ teaspoon garlic powder
½ teaspoon onion powder
½ teaspoon ground thyme
½ teaspoon ground oregano
1 jar (10 ounces) orange marmalade
2 tablespoons horseradish
3 tablespoons spicy brown mustard
½ teaspoon lemon rind, grated
¾ cup plus 2 tablespoons flour
¼ cup plus 2 tablespoons beer
1 egg, beaten
½ teaspoon baking powder
1 pound medium shrimp, shelled and deveined, leaving tails on
1 package (7 ounces) coconut
Oil for frying

Combine all spices, mix well and set aside. In a separate bowl, combine marmalade, horseradish, mustard and lemon rind. Chill. In a medium bowl, combine flour, beer, egg and baking powder. Mix well. Dip shrimp into seasoned mixture, shake off excess. Dip seasoned shrimp into beer batter. Dredge batter-coated shrimp in coconut.

Fry shrimp, five or six at a time in deep, 350° oil for 45 seconds on each side or until golden brown. Drain on paper towels. **Serves 2.**

Serve shrimp with orange sauce.

TUNA BURGERS

Christine E. Adams
St. Louis, MO

My brothers and sister and I loved Tuna Burgers which we often ate for a Friday night's dinner. Our mother would let us help her fix them. The melted cheese inside the Tuna Burger was delicious.

1 can (12¼ ounces) tuna
1 cup celery, chopped
½ cup yellow cheese, diced
1 small onion, minced
¼ cup mayonnaise
Salt and pepper to taste
6 hamburger buns

Mix all ingredients in a bowl. Fill hamburger buns with the tuna mixture. Wrap filled buns individually in waxed paper and heat on a baking sheet at 350° for 15 minutes. **Serves 6.**

Serve with spicy potato chips and carrot sticks.

LONE STAR TUNA CASSEROLE

Vicki Huberman
Dallas, TX

This recipe came from my grandmother.

My kids say, *"Mom makes awesome tuna casserole."*

1 onion, chopped
1 carton (8 ounces) fresh mushrooms, sliced
Olive oil
Cooking sherry
Salt and pepper
1 package (12 ounces) pasta
1 can cream of mushroom soup
1 can (12¼ ounces) tuna fish
4 cups Cheddar cheese, shredded

In a medium saucepan, sauté onion and mushrooms in olive oil and cooking sherry. Add a dash of salt and pepper. Prepare the pasta according to package directions and drain. In a 9x13-inch baking dish mix pasta, vegetables, soup and tuna. Sprinkle top with cheese and bake at 350° for 30 to 45 minutes, or until the cheese is melted. **Serves 12.**

Serve casserole with spinach salad and sourdough bread.

FISH WITH CRUMB-NUT TOPPING

Lynn M.
(Mrs. Donald S.) Osen
Laguna Beach, CA

I've found that most youngsters' lips go into zip lock mode when fish appears on the menu but the following recipe is welcomed by my grandchildren as well as grown-ups in the family. Like most successful recipes, it just grew over the years.

3 cups fresh bread crumbs
1 stick butter, melted
½ teaspoon salt
½ cup Parmesan cheese, freshly grated
1 tablespoon lemon peel, chopped
½ cup fresh parsley, chopped
1 tablespoon fresh basil, chopped
1 cup pine nuts or pecans, coarsely chopped
1 large fish (3 to 4 pounds) filleted

In mixing bowl, toss bread crumbs, butter, salt, Parmesan cheese, lemon peel, parsley and basil. Stir in nuts.

Place fish in buttered baking dish. Top with crumb mixture and bake in 350° oven for 20 to 30 minutes, depending upon size of fillet.

Either salmon or whitefish may be used. Mix may be prepared in advance and nuts added before baking. **Serves 4 to 6.**

Serve fish with garlic-roasted new potatoes.

SWISS CHEESE MUSHROOM PIE

Shirley Pruitt
Corona del Mar, CA

This twenty-year-old-recipe makes you a star. First, by its presentation and then the taste makes you appear to be a master chef. A golden brown lattice crust makes it look like it came from a French bakery. The requests for the recipe never stop, nor do the compliments.

3 tablespoons butter or margarine
1 cup onion, thinly sliced
1½ pounds mushrooms, sliced
1 teaspoon salt
Dash of pepper
½ teaspoon Worcestershire sauce
1 tablespoon lemon juice
1 package piecrust mix
½ pound Swiss cheese, shredded
2 egg yolks
1 tablespoon water

In a large skillet, melt butter or margarine over medium heat. Add onion and cook 2 minutes. Add mushrooms, salt, pepper, Worcestershire sauce and lemon juice. Cook 5 minutes, stirring occasionally. Drain mushroom mixture. Prepare pie crust according to package directions. Roll three-fourths of the dough into a 12-inch circle. Place dough in a 9-inch pie plate, allowing a 1-inch overhang. Roll out remaining dough and cut into 8 or 10 half-inch strips. Heat oven to 375°. Combine mushroom mixture and cheese. Mix well. Place into pastry shell. Arrange pastry strips, lattice fashion, on top of filling. Trim ends evenly with the edges of shell. Fold back overhanging dough and flute edges. Beat egg yolk and water and brush over pastry. Bake 35 to 40 minutes or until pastry is golden brown. Serve hot or cold. **Serves 6.**

Serve pie with your favorite steamed vegetables.

EGGPLANT NEAPOLITAN

Mrs. Kenneth Krasoff
Houston, TX

A wonderful meatless dinner entrée.

2 packages (12 ounces each) frozen spinach soufflé
1 eggplant, peeled and sliced
Vegetable or olive oil
2 eggs, beaten
1 carton (15 ounces) Ricotta cheese
1 cup Monterey Jack cheese, grated
1 cup Parmesan cheese, grated
1 can (15 ounces) tomato sauce with tomato bits
½ to 1 teaspoon Italian seasoning

Bake frozen spinach soufflé in preheated 350° oven for 30 minutes and set aside. Sauté eggplant in vegetable or olive oil until golden. Drain on paper towels. Beat eggs in electric mixer. Add Ricotta, Monterey Jack and Parmesan cheeses and mix well.

Grease 3-quart baking dish. Mix tomato sauce and Italian seasoning and spread into bottom of dish. Put in layer of eggplant slices. Spread cheese mixture over top of eggplant. Top with spinach soufflé, spreading evenly to cover cheese mixture. Bake uncovered in preheated 375° oven for 30 minutes. Can freeze either before or after baking. Defrost before baking. Consistency of dish looks loose before baking but firms up as baked. **Serves 8 to 10.**

Note: To make eggplant sweet, salt the slices and let them "sweat," then rinse before preparation for cooking.

Serve with Italian garlic bread—
a great vegetarian meal.

SAUTÉED POTATOES AND VEGGIES

Janet Swedburg
Axtell, NE

We enjoy this with the new potatoes raised in Nebraska. So good!

"Ugh!! More veggies."

3 tablespoons olive oil
4 medium baked potatoes, cubed
1 cup zucchini slices
1 cup red bell pepper, chopped
4 green onions, sliced
2 cloves garlic, minced
¼ cup parsley, chopped
1 lemon, grated rind
Salt and pepper to taste

Heat oil in 12-inch nonstick skillet over medium heat. Add potatoes, turning until brown and crisp. Add zucchini, peppers, onions and garlic, cook for 3 minutes. Stir in parsley and lemon rind, season with salt and pepper. **Serves 4.**

RICE ALFREDO

Lauren Henry
Fort Worth, TX

Despite the fact that my family is otherwise very picky, they always seem to enjoy this dish, especially with pork chops or roast pork.

4 tablespoons butter
1 cup half-and-half
3 cups rice, cooked
¾ cup Parmesan cheese, grated
1 can (4 ounces) sliced mushrooms, drained
2 tablespoons chives, chopped
¾ teaspoon seasoned pepper
1 teaspoon salt

Melt butter over medium heat. Add cream and allow to heat thoroughly, stirring constantly. Add rice, cheese, mushrooms, chives and seasonings. Toss lightly until most of the cream has been absorbed and rice is thoroughly heated. Serve immediately. **Serves 6.**

Serve with Daddy's Easy Parmigiana on page 115, and Italian bread sticks.

QUICK AND EASY POTATOES

Lynne Valentine
Balboa Island, CA

This is a great party recipe.

1 bag (2 pounds) frozen hash brown potatoes
1 can mushroom soup
1 pint sour cream
½ pound Cheddar cheese, shredded
Salt to taste
½ pound Cheddar cheese, shredded for top
2 tablespoons butter

Mix frozen hash brown potatoes, mushroom soup, sour cream and Cheddar cheese in a bowl and salt to taste. Spray 9x14-inch baking dish with nonstick cooking spray and pour mixture into dish. Sprinkle remaining cheese over the top. Dot with butter. Also can be made the night before. Bake at 350° for 45 minutes to 1 hour until top is brown. **Serves 8.**

Serve potatoes with Marinated Flank Steak on page 110, and rolls.

WHITE BEANS

Mrs. Leslie (Laquita) Price, Jr.
Tyronza, AR

This is our family's bean recipe and quite different from the ordinary.

1 pound GREAT NORTHERN® beans
3 to 4 ham hocks
1 can (28 ounces) crushed tomatoes
1 large onion, diced
Salt and pepper to taste
⅓ cup of ROTEL® tomatoes
1 can (11½ ounces) vegetable juice

In a large pot wash beans, drain, then add water to cover at least one inch above beans. Soak beans for 2 hours. Add ham hocks and leave the skin on until beans are ready to eat. Add the remaining ingredients. Cook on low heat for 2 hours. Check after 1 hour to see if extra liquid is needed. **Serves 6 to 8.**

Serve beans with hot buttered corn bread.

SPINACH AND STRAWBERRY SALAD

Barbara Alexander
Batavia, IL

Looks pretty, tastes sweet. The kids always loved this.

Salad:

1 pound spinach, washed, dried and torn

1 teaspoon fresh dill, chopped

1 teaspoon sesame seeds, toasted

1 pint fresh strawberries, sliced in half

Dressing:

½ cup salad oil

¼ cup red wine vinegar

¼ cup sugar

¼ teaspoon garlic powder

¼ teaspoon onion powder

¼ teaspoon dry mustard

¼ teaspoon salt and pepper or to taste

Toss salad ingredients together. Make dressing and shake well. Add just before serving. **Serves 6 to 8.**

Serve salad with Fish with Crumb-Nut Topping on page 124.

ORANGE-MINT TOMATO SAUCE

Lauren Hutton
New York, NY

I discovered this recipe on the volcanic island of Pantelleria off Sicily, where very few things can grow. The winds are so strong that orange trees are grown inside a ten-foot-high rock wall. Almost every house has its own orange tree corral.

2 tablespoons olive oil

½ orange

½ teaspoon red pepper flakes

1 can (16 ounces) peeled Italian tomatoes

2 teaspoons large capers

10 to 15 large mint leaves

1 cup water

In a large skillet, heat olive oil. Place orange half sliced side down in the heated oil. Sprinkle red pepper over oil and brown. Add tomatoes, capers, mint leaves and water. Add salt and pepper to taste. Stir and simmer 30 minutes. While simmering watch carefully and add extra water if needed. **Serves 2.**

Serve over favorite pasta.

CHEESY CORN CHOWDER

Mara Squar
Tarzana, CA

I don't remember if this recipe comes from the newspaper or a magazine. I do know that my kids have always loved coming home to a pot of this soup for lunch (even if lunch was after school!) The important thing to them is the EXTRA CHEESE. Sometimes it ends up with two very full cups of cheese if they're around to help.

1 can (16 ounces) whole kernel corn
2 medium potatoes, peeled and diced
3 cups chicken broth
1 cup celery, chopped
½ teaspoon TABASCO® sauce
Salt to taste
2 tablespoons butter
3 tablespoons flour
2 cups milk
1¼ cups Cheddar cheese, shredded
1 red pepper, diced

Combine corn, potatoes, broth, celery and TABASCO® sauce in a large stock pot. Season to taste with salt and heat to boiling. Cover and simmer 30 minutes or until potatoes are tender.

Melt butter in a heavy saucepan and stir in flour. Cook, stirring, just long enough for flour to absorb butter but do not brown. Add milk and cook, stirring, until the mixture comes to a boil and thickens. Add to corn mixture. Stir in cheese and red pepper. Cook over low heat until the cheese melts and the mixture is thoroughly heated. **Serves 8.**

Serve garnished with cooked, crumbled bacon or cooked, diced ham.

GAZPACHO HOME-STYLE

Mr. & Mrs.
Ben R. Weber, Jr.
Dallas, TX

For moms who have a hard time getting their children to eat vegetables, fix this soup: they will be begging for more!

"I did not know vegetables could taste like this!"

1 (10¾ ounces) can CAMPBELL'S® Italian Tomato soup
1½ cups bottled Bloody Mary mix
1¼ cups water
½ to 1 cup cucumber, chopped
½ to 1 cup tomato, chopped
½ cup green pepper, chopped
½ cup yellow pepper, chopped
½ cup Spanish onion, chopped
2 tablespoons olive oil
2 tablespoons red wine vinegar
1 tablespoon commercial Italian dressing
1 tablespoon lemon juice
2 cloves garlic, minced
Dash of salt and pepper
½ teaspoon hot sauce
⅛ teaspoon garlic salt
⅛ teaspoon Worcestershire sauce

Combine all ingredients in a large bowl. Chill at least six hours, even though it will taste great in an hour if you are in a hurry. Store in an air-tight container in the refrigerator.
Serves 8 to 10.

Serve gazpacho with Italian bread sticks.

CHAPTER FIVE

WHO'S FOR DESSERT?

Everybody! Desserts could easily have been half the recipes in the book, but we had to stop somewhere, and these were the best we've seen in many a year. (Maybe next time we'll do a recipe book that's all desserts.) We have discovered that not only is dessert a big incentive to clean plates, but oftentimes the most memorable part of any meal. Why else would restaurants ply us so with the pastry cart? Dessert can be simple like Elton John's Rice Pudding, which must be very comforting after a piano-pounding concert. But, one thing we learned in our first book, *Pure & Simple,* is proven once again. Chocolate reigns forever.

CHOCOLATE CHIP SURPRISE CAKE

Melinda Jayson
Dallas, TX

This cake remains popular with all the kids, including the ones who've grown up.

"A cake with chocolate chips in it is fun to eat."

Cake:

1½ cups boiling water
1 cup dates, chopped
1 teaspoon baking soda
¼ cup butter
¼ cup vegetable shortening
1¼ cups sugar
2 eggs
2 cups flour
¾ teaspoon baking soda
¾ teaspoon salt

Topping:

1 package (6 ounces) chocolate chips
½ cup sugar
½ cups nuts, chopped

Frosting:

2 tablespoons butter, melted
2 squares chocolate, melted
2 cups powdered sugar
1 teaspoon vanilla extract
½ teaspoon salt
¼ cup milk

Cake: Preheat oven to 350°. Grease and flour a 13x9x2-inch pan.* Pour boiling water over dates and add 1 teaspoon baking soda; let cool. Cream butter, shortening and sugar. Add eggs, date mixture, flour, the ¾ teaspoon of baking soda and salt. Blend well. Pour batter into pan. The surprise in this cake is the rich flavor of the dates. Combine topping ingredients and sprinkle topping over batter. Bake for 40 minutes. Cool and frost.

* This cake also can be baked in two 8-inch layer pans at 325° for 40 minutes, and left to cool for 10 minutes before removing from the pans. If you choose this method, just frost the sides of the cake.

Frosting: Combine butter and chocolate. Add powdered sugar, vanilla extract, salt and milk. Stir until proper consistency to spread.

Cut into squares to serve. **Serves 8 to 10.**

Serve cake with chilled coffee or cold milk.

CRUNCH CAKE

Susan Goldfarb
Brentwood, TN

This recipe is from my children's grandmother, who is a great cook and baker. Once baked, it does not last long. You might say the kids simply inhale it!

Topping:

2 tablespoons butter
¼ cup sugar
½ cup powdered sugar
¼ cup graham cracker crumbs
½ cup nuts, finely chopped

Cake:

4 egg whites
1 teaspoon cream of tartar
½ cup sugar
1 cup butter
1 cup sugar
4 egg yolks
2 teaspoons vanilla extract
2½ cups flour
½ teaspoon baking soda
¼ teaspoon baking powder
⅛ teaspoon mace
½ teaspoon salt
½ cup milk

Topping: Mix together butter, sugar, powdered sugar, graham cracker crumbs and nuts. Pat into bottom of tube pan.

Cake: Beat egg whites with cream of tartar until almost stiff and then beat in ½ cup sugar. Continue beating until peaks form; set aside. For cake batter, cream butter and 1 cup sugar until light and fluffy. Add egg yolks and vanilla and beat thoroughly. Sift dry ingredients together and add alternately with milk in thirds, beating until smooth after each addition. Fold cake batter and beaten egg whites together until blended. Pour batter over topping/crunch mixture. Bake at 350° for 50 minutes to 1 hour. Let cool 10 to 15 minutes and loosen cake edges with knife. Invert cake onto serving plate. **Serves 8 to 10.**

Serve cake with frozen yogurt sprinked with nuts.

BLACK ANGEL FOOD CAKE

Susan Z. Diamond
Melrose Park, IL

The recipe is from my aunt and was a childhood favorite of mine. Since our *"children"* are the four-legged kind, I have no kid quote for you, but the cake is always a hit with our niece and nephew.

½ cup cocoa
1¾ cups sugar, sifted
12 egg whites
1½ teaspoons cream of tartar
1 cup cake flour, sifted
¼ teaspoon almond extract
¾ teaspoon vanilla extract

Sift cocoa and sugar together 3 times. Beat egg whites until foamy. Sprinkle cream of tartar on top and beat until stiff. Fold in cocoa and sugar mixture. Fold in flour. Add flavorings. Gently pour into angel food cake pan with bottom of pan covered with waxed paper. Bake at 350° for 45 minutes. **Serves 8.**

Note: For best results, sift ingredients several times before measuring. Your result is a much lighter cake.

Serve cake with chocolate sauce and coffee or cold milk.

MILLION-DOLLAR ANGEL FOOD CAKE

Katherine B. Madden
Dayton, OH

6 tablespoons chocolate syrup
6 tablespoons sugar
⅛ teaspoon salt
2½ pints whipping cream
1 angel food cake, baked

Combine chocolate syrup, sugar and salt with whipping cream and place in refrigerator for at least 4 hours or overnight. You can buy a cake or use a boxed cake mix. Remove the chocolate mix from the refrigerator and whip to a spreading consistency. Cut angel food cake in half and ice top of bottom half of cake. Place top half of cake on the icing and ice the outside of the cake. **Serves 8 to 10.**

Serve cake with hot coffee or cold milk.

CARAMEL CAKE

Ben & Julie Crenshaw
Austin, TX

My mother used to make this and now I make it for the whole family to enjoy—from Claire, who is only one year old, to Katherine, who is 5½, and my husband Ben, as well. It's incredibly rich and gooey, and also incredibly easy to make.

"I love to poke the holes in it." Katherine Crenshaw

1 box chocolate cake mix
1 can (14 ounces) sweetened condensed milk
1 jar (10 ounces) caramel topping
1 container (8 ounces) whipped topping

Prepare cake mix as directed. Bake in a 9x13-inch pan. When cake is finished baking, take the end of a wooden spoon and poke holes over the entire cake. Pour condensed milk and caramel into the holes. After cooling, cover the cake with foil and refrigerate for 3 hours or overnight. When you are ready to eat, spread whipped cream over the cake and serve. **Serves 10 to 12.**

Serve with a tall glass of cold milk.

DIRT CAKE

Linda Tondu
Houston, TX

This is my own version of my sister-in-law Mary Marzec's recipe that her daughter's Brownie Troop served at a campout. My kids love to help make the Dirt Cake. They especially like finding the hidden *"worms."*

1 package (1 pound) OREO® cookies
1 package (8 ounces) cream cheese
1 cup powdered sugar
2 packages (3½ ounces each) instant vanilla or chocolate pudding
3½ cups milk
1 carton (12 ounces) frozen whipped topping
2 packages GUMMI WORMS®

Put cookies in a plastic bag and crush. Soften cream cheese and cream with powdered sugar. Combine pudding, milk and frozen whipped topping; add to creamed mixture. Reserve 1 to 2 cups of the cookies. Combine remaining cookies and some GUMMI WORMS® with creamed mixture. Pour mixture into an 8-inch flower pot, 10-inches deep with no drainage hole, which you can sterilize by boiling. If you prefer, eight to ten individual serving-sized flower pots can be used. Sprinkle remaining crushed cookies on top. Refrigerate for 2 hours. Decorate with more GUMMI WORMS® and plastic flowers. **Serves 8 to 10.**

Serve cake with chilled fruit juice.

DO-IT-MYSELF CAKE

Anne Marie Morton
Houston, TX

My best friend, Denise Martinez, confided this recipe to me after it received rave reviews at a baby shower she was hosting. My four-year-old loves to help in the kitchen, but, with a new baby, I don't always have the time to supervise her as closely as most recipes require. This recipe needs minimal supervision, with an older child no supervision at all, and no chance of eggshell in the batter!

Cake:

1 Devil's Food cake mix, and 1 can (1 pound 4 ounces) cherry pie filling, OR:
1 spice cake mix, and 1 can (1 pound 4 ounces) apple pie filling
Powdered sugar, for dusting

Chocolate Drizzle:

1½ cups powdered sugar
¼ cup cocoa
¼ cup butter, softened
5 to 6 tablespoons milk

Cake: Generously spray a BUNDT® pan with nonstick cooking spray. Preheat oven to 350°. Hand mix the two ingredients until cake mix is well moistened. Pour into prepared BUNDT® pan. Bake for 45 to 50 minutes. **Serves 6 to 8.**

Chocolate Drizzle: Mix together powdered sugar, cocoa, butter and milk. Drizzle on warm chocolate cake.

Dust spice cake with powdered sugar.

Serve chocolate cake warm with cherry vanilla ice cream. Serve spice cake with a premium vanilla ice cream.

HOT FUDGE CAKE

Zita Lefebure
Beverly Hills, CA

The Hot Fudge Cake is a favorite of all three of my children.

"It is deliciouser than a hot fudge sundae and a warm brownie smooshed together." Stephen Lefebure (age 4).

¾ cup sugar
2 tablespoons butter, melted
½ teaspoon salt
1 cup flour
4 teaspoons cocoa
2 teaspoons baking powder
½ teaspoon vanilla extract
½ cup milk
½ cup brown sugar
½ cup sugar
5 tablespoons cocoa
1 cup cold water
½ cup nuts, chopped (optional)

Mix together butter, sugar and salt. Sift together flour, cocoa and baking powder. Add vanilla to milk. Add milk and dry ingredients alternately to first mixture. Add nuts if desired. Spread batter in well-greased square pan. Mix brown sugar, sugar and remaining cocoa. Sprinkle over the batter, pour cold water over the mixture and bake at 350° for 40 minutes. **Serves 8 to 10.**

Serve hot with vanilla ice cream.

MALGAMATION CAKE

William R. Jones
New York, NY

This is *"southern short"* for Amalgamation Cake, meaning a cake comprised of an amalgamation of whatever can be found in the cupboard. It dates back to the Civil War when the contents of one's cupboard were unpredictable. Thus the ingredients often changed. My mother has made many modifications over the years. It is a Southerner's answer to the fruitcake. It's always around the house during the holidays and seems to be well-received by Yankees as well. It's even better with homemade wine.

Cake:

2¼ cups sugar
1¼ cups shortening
3 cups flour, sifted
Pinch salt
3 teaspoons baking powder
6 egg whites, stiffly beaten
1 teaspoon vanilla extract

Frosting and Filling:

6 egg yolks, well beaten
1¼ cups sugar
1 cup milk
¾ cup unsalted butter
1 cup English walnuts or pecans, chopped
½ cup golden raisins, finely chopped
¼ cup sweet red wine, more to taste or to adjust consistency of filling if necessary
1 carton candied red and green cherries, for garnish
1 cup flaked coconut, for garnish

Cake: Grease and prepare three 9-inch cake pans with shortening, dusting lightly with flour. Preheat oven to 325°. Cream together sugar and shortening until fluffy. Sift together flour, salt and baking powder. Add slowly to creamed mixture alternately with milk. Fold in stiffly beaten egg whites and vanilla. Bake for 25 minutes or until lightly browned and sides are beginning to pull away from the pans. Cool on wire racks. Dust off loose crumbs before frosting.

Frosting and Filling: Mix together egg yolks, sugar and milk in heavy saucepan. Stir constantly over medium-high heat. Cook until thickened. Add butter. Stir well to incorporate butter thoroughly. Remove from heat. Stir in nuts, raisins and wine. Frost each layer and the sides with icing. Decorate with candied red and green cherries and coconut. Keep refrigerated. May be frozen for six months in an airtight container. **Serves 10 to 12.**

MARBLE CAKE

Mitchell Yoffe
Stamford, CT

This Marble Cake is an original scrumptious recipe that has been handed down for three generations (since my great-grandmother).

"You never have to wash the bowl; we lick it clean."

½ pound butter
1 cup sugar
1 teaspoon vanilla extract
5 eggs
2 cups flour
2 teaspoons baking powder
⅓ cup NESTLÉ® QUIK® chocolate powder

Cream the butter and the sugar. Add vanilla. Beat in one egg at a time. Combine flour and baking soda, and add to cream mixture. Stir well. Grease the cake pan. Pour one-third of dough into the cake pan. Pour another one-third into an extra bowl. Mix ⅓ cup of chocolate powder into the remaining one-third batter. Pour the chocolate mixture on top of one-third of the dough in the cake pan. Put the remaining one-third batter on top of the chocolate mixture. Use a fork in an up-and-down motion to mix the mixture in the cake pan, then bake at 350° for 1 hour. **Serves 8 to 10.**

Serve with whipped cream dusted with chocolate powder.

MISSISSIPPI-MUD CAKE

Elizabeth Scarff
Jackson, MS

When we moved to Jackson from Dallas, we found that Mississippi people take food very seriously—they talk about food and restaurants constantly. Even so, when I make this cake I am constantly asked for the recipe, and when I give it, the comment I receive is that it always tastes better when I make it.

Cake:

1 cup margarine, melted
2 cups sugar
4 eggs
1½ cups flour
½ cup cocoa
1 can (3½ ounces) coconut
1 cup pecans, chopped

Topping:

1 jar (7 ounces) marshmallow cream
½ cup evaporated milk or ¼ cup plain milk
1 box powdered sugar
1 tablespoon vanilla extract
⅓ cup cocoa
6 tablespoons margarine, softened

Cake: Combine margarine with sugar and eggs. Combine flour, cocoa, coconut and pecans in a bowl and mix well. Blend thoroughly with sugar and egg mixture. Pour cake batter into a greased and floured 9x13-inch pan. Bake at 350° for 30 minutes.

Topping: While cake is still hot, spread on marshmallow cream. While cake is cooling, combine evaporated milk or plain milk, powdered sugar, vanilla, cocoa and margarine. Let cake cool, then spread with topping. Refrigerate until chilled and then cut into squares. Keep refrigerated. **Serves 10 to 12.**

Serve cake with vanilla frozen yogurt.

MOTHER'S CHEESECAKE

Joan Fey
Atlanta, GA

I have made this wonderful, light cake for holidays and birthdays when everyone in the family was at home.

"Mom, this is the best you've ever made."

Crust:

1 package (5⅓ ounces) graham crackers, crushed

¼ cup sugar

¼ cup plus 2 tablespoons butter, melted in springform pan

2 packages (8 ounces each) cream cheese

1 cup sugar

5 eggs, separated

1 teaspoon lemon juice

1 teaspoon vanilla extract

1 pint sour cream

Combine graham crackers, sugar and butter. Mix well. Firmly press crust into bottom of 9-inch pan. Cream sugar and cheese until light and fluffy. Add egg yolks, then flavorings and sour cream. Mix thoroughly. Beat egg whites until shiny and stiff. Do not overbeat. Carefully fold egg whites into cheese batter. Pour batter onto crust. Bake at 300°, beginning with a cold oven, for 1 hour. Turn oven off and leave for 1 hour. Crack oven door for another ½ hour. **Serves 6 to 8.**

Note: Should be made the day before serving. *Use fresh strawberries with a glaze, crushed pineapple, blueberries, cherries or fruit of your choice for the topping.*

SNOW-ON-THE-MOUNTAIN CAKE

Nancy Skuble
Santa Monica, CA

My mother made this special cake when we were celebrating someone's special accomplishment.

Cake:

8 whole eggs
2 cups sugar
½ teaspoon salt
4 teaspoons vanilla extract
1 cup flour
2 teaspoons baking powder
2 cups nuts, finely chopped into small pieces
2 pound package pitted dates, chopped into small pieces

Topping:

11 medium oranges, peeled and cut into pieces
9 medium bananas, peeled and cut into pieces
2 pints whipping cream, whipped
1½ boxes ANGEL FLAKE® coconut

Mix eggs, sugar, salt and vanilla. Mix flour and baking powder and sprinkle over the nuts and dates. Combine the egg mixture and nut mixture. Place in two cake pans or one oblong pan, which have been sprayed with nonstick cooking spray and dusted with flour. Bake in 350° oven for 30 minutes. When cake is finished baking, the batter will be half an inch high. Do not expect the cake to be the height of the cake pan.

After cake has cooled, cut (or tear) into bite-sized pieces. Place about 25 squares of the cake close together on the bottom of a fancy cake plate. Cover cake with fruit and make mountain-like shape. Cover with whipped cream. Decorate with coconut. Refrigerate for 8 hours.
Serves 10 to 12.

Serve cake with iced mint tea.

COOKIE CHEESECAKE

Evelyn W. Weissman
Lawrence, NY

This cheesecake almost melts in your mouth.

½ package OREO® cookies (21), crushed
4 tablespoons butter
4 packages (8 ounces each) cream cheese
1¼ cups sugar
2 tablespoons flour
4 eggs, plus 3 yolks
½ package OREO® cookies (21), broken, not crushed
2 cups sour cream
¼ cup sugar

Combine 21 crushed cookies with melted butter and press into a 9-inch springform pan which has been sprayed with nonstick cooking spray. Combine cream cheese, sugar, flour, eggs and yolks. Place one-half of the cream cheese mixture on the cookie base. Place the other 21 cookies, (broken, not crushed) on top of mixture. Pour on the other half of cream mixture. In a 225° oven, bake for 25 minutes. Make topping by mixing sour cream with ¼ cup sugar. Remove cake and increase oven temperature to 350°. Add topping and bake for 7 minutes. Remove from oven after cake is cool and place in refrigerator until firm. **Serves 8 to 10.**

Serve cheesecake with favorite hot tea.

SOUR CREAM COFFEE CAKE

Georgia S. Davis
Dallas, TX

Coffee Cake:
1 cup margarine
2 cups sugar
2 eggs
1 cup sour cream
¼ teaspoon vanilla extract
2 cups flour
1 teaspoon baking powder
¼ teaspoon salt

Topping:
½ cup nuts, chopped
1 teaspoon cinnamon
½ cup brown sugar
Powdered sugar, for sifting

Cream margarine; gradually add sugar and mix well. Add eggs, one at a time, beating well after each addition. Fold in sour cream and vanilla. Stir in dry ingredients. Spoon half of the batter into a greased and floured BUNDT® pan. Combine topping ingredients and sprinkle half of the topping over the batter. Repeat with remaining batter and topping. Bake at 350° for 50 minutes. Cool for 15 minutes before removing from pan. Sprinkle with powdered sugar. Let stand a day before serving. **Serves 8 to 10.**

SPICE CAKE

Stan Richards
Dallas, TX

This was my son Grant's favorite cake when he was three. At age thirty-two, it still is. And now he has two boys of his own who are big fans of the Spice Cake. Maybe there's a Spice Cake gene.

1 cup water
1 cup raisins
¾ cup cooking oil
1½ cups sugar
3 eggs
2½ cups flour
1¼ teaspoons baking soda
½ teaspoon cloves
1 teaspoon allspice
1 teaspoon nutmeg
1 cup pecans, chopped
1 cup powdered sugar, sifted
1 lemon, juiced

In a small saucepan, combine water and raisins. Bring to a boil. Remove from heat. In a separate mixing bowl, combine raisin mixture with oil and sugar. Cool. Add eggs, flour, baking soda, cloves, allspice, nutmeg, cinnamon and pecans. Bake in a tube pan at 325° for 50 minutes. Let cool in pan for 10 minutes. While cake is cooling, mix together sugar and lemon juice. Remove cake from pan and pour lemon glaze over cake. **Serves 12.**

TOMATO SOUP CAKE

Ingrid Curtiss, M.D.
Los Angeles, CA

This recipe is a part of World War II history when butter, shortening, etc., were all rationed. Since *"ganna and gampa"* didn't have butter for cakes, they baked recipes like this that didn't require much butter.

In answer to what's your favorite vegetable? *"Tomato Soup Cake."* Jon-Robert

Cake:

1 cup sugar
2 tablespoons butter
1½ cups flour
1 teaspoon soda
1 teaspoon cinnamon
1 teaspoon nutmeg
1 cup raisins, floured
1 cup nuts, chopped
1 can tomato soup

Frosting:

1 cup powdered sugar
1 tablespoon butter
1 package (8 ounces) cream cheese

Cream sugar and butter. Add flour, soda, cinnamon, nutmeg, raisins, nuts and tomato soup to the creamed mixture. Pour batter into cake pan which has been sprayed with nonstick cooking spray. Bake 35 to 40 minutes at 375°.

While cake is cooling, combine frosting ingredients and blend thoroughly. Spread on top of cooled cake. **Serves 8 to 10.**

Serve cake with hot spiced cinnamon tea.

TORTE

Gloria Nycek
Dearborn, MI

This is an old Polish recipe.

Cake:

10 eggs, separated
1 cup powdered sugar
½ teaspoon almond extract
1 cup nuts, ground
1 cup rye bread or biscuits, dried and ground

Filling:

5 whole eggs
1 cup sugar
1 cup plus 2 tablespoons butter
1 teaspoon baking powder
1 teaspoon instant coffee or cocoa
2 teaspoons water

Cake: Separate egg yolks from whites. Combine yolks with powdered sugar until white. Toward end of this combining, add the almond extract. Mix the nuts with the bread and baking powder. Add to yolk mixture. Beat egg whites until stiff and fold into egg and nut mixture. Stir lightly and pour into a pan which has been buttered and lightly sprinkled with bread crumbs. Bake at a temperature of 200° for 45 minutes.

Filling: Beat 5 whole eggs with sugar in a double boiler, stirring until thickened. Cool this mixture, stirring occasionally. Cream butter and combine with the cooled egg mixture. Add the coffee or cocoa dissolved in a little water. Cut torte into 3 layers. Brush each layer with a flavored liqueur mixed with water. Place filling between each layer and chill. **Serves 8 to 10.**

Serve Torte with hot coffee and mocha cream.

APRICOT PASTRIES

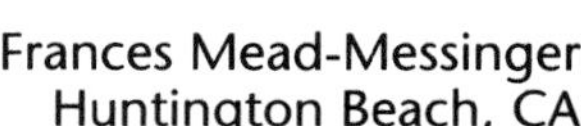

Frances Mead-Messinger
Huntington Beach, CA

The following recipe was a favorite of my children and now is a favorite of my grandchildren. In 1991, my daughter (now thirty-five) entered the recipe in the Napa County Fair and won First Prize. And it is so easy!

2 cups dried apricots
2 cups water
3 cups flour, sifted
1 tablespoon sugar
½ teaspoon salt
1 cup shortening
½ cup milk
1 package active dry yeast
Powdered sugar

Simmer 2 cups dried apricots in 2 cups water until tender. Let cool. Sift together the flour, sugar and salt. Cut shortening into the flour mixture. Scald the milk, cool to warm, and add the yeast and let soften. Add to flour mixture and mix well.

Divide dough into four parts. On a surface well-dusted with powdered sugar, roll out one part at a time to a 10-inch square. Cut each square into sixteen, 2½-inch squares and place a heaping teaspoonful of the stewed apricots into the center of each square. Pinch the two opposite corners together. Place 2 inches apart on a greased cookie sheet and let stand 10 minutes.

Bake in a 350° oven 10 to 12 minutes. Remove immediately from pan and cool on rack. Sprinkle with powdered sugar. **Makes about 5 dozen.**

Note: These freeze beautifully; however, do not roll in the sugar or sprinkle with sugar before freezing. Remove from freezer and let stand for 15 minutes. Follow previous directions for baking. If you wish to bake them before freezing, just thaw them in a warm oven to serve and then sprinkle with the sugar.

Serve pastries as a brunch item on a buffet.

CHOCOLATE SOUFFLÉ

Marlo Thomas
New York, NY

This is a recipe that I love and I think children will also love.

Marlo Thomas carries on the tradition of her father, the late Danny Thomas, in her support of St. Jude Children's Research Hospital, which he founded.

2 tablespoons butter
2 tablespoons flour
¾ cup milk
Pinch of salt
2 squares unsweetened chocolate
⅓ cup sugar
2 tablespoons cold coffee
½ teaspoon vanilla extract
3 egg yolks, lightly beaten
4 egg whites, stiffly beaten
Whipped cream

In a saucepan, melt the butter, add the flour and stir with a wire whisk until blended. Meanwhile, bring the milk to a boil and add all at once to the butter-flour mixture, stirring vigorously with the whisk. Add pinch of salt.

Melt the chocolate with the sugar and coffee over hot water. Stir the melted chocolate mixture into the sauce and add the vanilla. Beat in the egg yolks, one at a time, and cool.

Fold in the stiffly beaten egg whites and turn the mixture into a buttered 2-quart casserole sprinkled with sugar. Bake at 375° for 35 to 45 minutes, or until puffed and brown. **Serves 6.**

Serve immediately with whipped cream.

PEANUT BUTTER CUPCAKES

Betty (Mrs. William) Seitz
Dallas, TX

My elderly aunt made these cupcakes for dozens of children in our family through the years. The children always loved this recipe and remembered it when they grew up and had children of their own. My two boys (college students) love it when I send these in a college care package.

⅓ cup butter
1 cup brown sugar, packed
½ cup peanut butter
2 eggs
½ cup brown sugar, packed
1½ teaspoons vanilla extract
2 cups flour
½ teaspoon salt
2 teaspoons baking powder
¾ cup milk

Preheat oven to 350°. Beat butter until soft and blend in 1 cup of brown sugar until graininess disappears. Add peanut butter, eggs, remaining ½ cup brown sugar and vanilla and beat until light and fluffy. Sift flour, salt and baking powder into the mixture. Beat well. Add milk. Pour into lightly greased or paper-lined 12-cup muffin pan. Bake about 25 minutes. Ice with maple syrup drizzled over cupcakes while still warm from oven. **Makes 1 dozen.**

Serve cupcakes with cold milk.

KISS COOKIES

Mrs. Joan A. Stewart
Houston, TX

My husband Dale gave me this recipe from his mother when we were first married. Our daughter Alexandra, brings these cookies to her class at school to celebrate her November birthday. She never has any left to bring back home.

"My mom never lets me have enough."

1¾ cups flour
1 teaspoon baking soda
½ teaspoon salt
½ cup sugar
½ cup light brown sugar, packed
½ cup shortening
½ cup, plus 1 tablespoon creamy peanut butter
1 egg
2 tablespoons milk
1 teaspoon vanilla extract
1 large bag HERSHEY'S® KISSES®, unwrapped

Mix flour, soda and salt together. In a separate bowl, combine sugars, shortening, peanut butter, egg, milk and vanilla extract. Mix at medium speed until combined. Add dry ingredients and mix well. Chill dough for 1 hour.

Preheat oven to 375°. Roll dough into 1-inch balls. Roll in sugar. Place on a cookie sheet and bake for 10 minutes. Immediately press an unwrapped chocolate kiss into center of each cookie. **Makes 2 dozen.**

Serve cookies with cold milk.

MOLASSES COOKIES

Patricia A. Goff
McLean, VA

This recipe was given to me by a friend over twenty years ago and has been my favorite all-around cookie recipe ever since. I can always count on this one to be well-received by both young and old. I never have to worry about having any left over.

"Who ate the last cookie?"

¾ cup shortening
1 cup sugar
¼ cup molasses
1 egg
2 cups flour, sifted
2 teaspoons baking soda
½ teaspoon ground cloves
½ teaspoon ground ginger
1 teaspoon ground cinnamon
½ teaspoon salt
Sugar, for rolling

Melt shortening in a 3-quart saucepan over low heat. Remove from heat and let cool. Add sugar, molasses and egg. Beat well. Sift together flour, soda and spices. Add to sugar mixture and mix well. Form into 1-inch balls. Roll in sugar and place on greased cookie sheet two inches apart. Bake at 375° for 8 to 10 minutes.
Makes 3 dozen.

Place frozen yogurt between two cookies for miniature ice cream sandwiches.

NUTTIEST CHOCOLATE-CHOCOLATE CHIP COOKIES

Marcialea Rittenberg
Marina del Rey, CA

My children helped me put this recipe together and it is very special to me. Whenever I make a batch, my neighbors and friends can't wait to have some.

"Mom, all of my friends want your recipe!"

2 squares unsweetened chocolate, melted
¾ cup butter, softened
½ cup sugar
1 egg, beaten
1 teaspoon vanilla extract
¼ cup milk
½ cup powdered sugar
2 cups flour
1 teaspoon baking powder
1 package (6 ounces) chocolate chips
¾ cup pecans or walnuts, chopped

Heat oven to 350°. Melt chocolate squares. In a large bowl combine chocolate, butter, sugar, egg, vanilla and milk. Cream until smooth. Add the flour and baking powder and stir to combine. Stir chocolate chips and nuts into batter, mixing thoroughly. Drop by spoonfuls onto greased cookie sheet and bake for 8 to 10 minutes. **Makes 2 dozen.**

When cookies are cool, add your favorite vanilla or chocolate frosting and top with colored candy sprinkles.

OUR HAPPY CHILDHOOD FAVORITES

Marian Marshall
New York, NY

From my mother, memories of my childhood with my sister. They were always served with milk.

1 cup soft shortening
2 cups brown sugar, packed
2 eggs
½ cup cold coffee
3½ cups flour
1 teaspoon baking soda
1 teaspoon salt
1 teaspoon nutmeg
1 teaspoon cinnamon
⅛ teaspoon instant coffee crystals
2½ cups raisins
¾ cup walnuts, chopped
¾ cup pecans, chopped
1 tablespoon sour cream

Cream together the shortening, brown sugar and eggs. Stir in ½ cup cold coffee. Set aside.

Sift together the dry ingredients and add to the shortening mixture. Mix in the raisins, nuts and sour cream.

Chill dough for 2 hours before baking. Drop rounded tablespoons of dough, 2 inches apart on lightly greased baking sheet. Sprinkle with nuts. Bake at 400° for 8 to 10 minutes or until lightly browned. Remove from baking sheets and set aside to cool. **Makes 4 dozen.**

Serve cookies with iced coffee or cold milk.

PAPA PETE'S OATMEAL COOKIES

Mrs. Barry Bailey
Fort Worth, TX

From Grandfather Papa Pete's (Dr. Barry Bailey) cooking.

1¼ cups butter
¾ cup brown sugar, firmly packed
½ cup sugar
1 egg
1 teaspoon vanilla extract
⅛ cup milk
1½ cups flour
1 teaspoon baking soda
1 teaspoon salt
1 teaspoon cinnamon
2 cups raisins
3 cups rolled oats

Heat oven to 375°. Mix butter and sugars well. Beat in egg, vanilla and milk. Add combined flour, baking soda, salt and spices; mix well. Stir in raisins, then oats. Drop by tablespoonfuls onto ungreased cookie sheet. Bake 11 minutes. **Makes 3 dozen.**

Put a small scoop of vanilla ice cream between two cookies for a delicious ice cream sandwich.

SUGAR CLOUDS

Patti Estabrooks
Laguna Beach, CA

My daughter loved these when she was a little girl. Now I send them to her in college. You can never outgrow the sweet taste of Sugar Clouds.

8 egg whites, room temperature
¼ teaspoon salt
1½ cups sugar
2 teaspoons vanilla extract
1 teaspoon vinegar
1 tablespoon cornstarch, sifted

Preheat oven to 400°. Beat egg whites with salt until frothy. Add sugar and vanilla slowly and beat until stiff. Fold in vinegar and cornstarch. Spread clouds into freestanding shapes on a cookie sheet sprayed with nonstick cooking spray. Reduce oven temperature to 250°. Bake for 1½ hours. **Serves 6.**

For variations, add chocolate, coconut, lemon or peppermint extract to mixture when beating. Top with sprinkles, cinnamon or your favorite fruit.

DAVE'S BROWNIES

Doug McNeill
Four Seasons Hotel
Washington, D.C.

1¾ sticks butter
⅔ cup shortening
9 squares (1 ounce each) bitter chocolate
3⅓ cups sugar
Pinch of salt
4 eggs
2½ cups flour
2½ cups walnuts, chopped or ground
1 teaspoon vanilla

Preheat oven to 350°. In a saucepan, over medium heat, melt together butter, shortening and bitter chocolate. After combining, remove from heat. Place double boiler on the stove with water in the bottom part and to the top part, add eggs, sugar and salt. Now turn the heat on to a low setting and, when mixture is warm, whip to a fluffy consistency. Take off heat and transfer to another pot. Next, fold flour into the egg mixture, stirring gently. Do NOT overmix. Add vanilla. Now add the chocolate mixture to the flour and egg mixture and mix gently, until batter is smooth. Place batter into a greased or parchment paper-lined pan, 18x12½x1-inch. Bake 20 minutes or until brownies feel just slightly soft in the center. Remove from the oven and, while warm, cut into two-inch squares. When cooled, separate and enjoy!
Makes 4 to 5 dozen.

GOLD MEDAL BROWNIES

Bruce Jenner
Malibu, CA

This is the first thing my wife Kris ever made for me and it was love at first bite. Ever since, these have been a regular feature around our house—especially at Christmastime. They disappear fast, so I've just learned to make them myself.

"A perfect snack to sneak in the middle of the night."

2 sticks of butter
4 squares (1 ounce each) unsweetened chocolate
4 eggs
2 teaspoons vanilla extract
2 cups sugar
½ teaspoon salt
½ teaspoon baking powder
1 cup flour
1 cup walnuts, chopped
1 package (12 ounces) miniature chocolate chips
½ teaspoon salt

Slowly melt butter and unsweetened chocolate over low heat in saucepan. Set aside. In food processor, using the regular chopping blade, blend eggs with vanilla. Add sugar, salt, baking powder and flour through feeding tube. Add chocolate mixture through the feeding tube. Let mix for a few seconds until thoroughly blended. With pulse or on-and-off method, blend in nuts and chips. Pour into greased 9x11-inch pan and bake at 325° for 25 minutes or until done. Let cool and cut into squares. **Serves 10 to 12.**

Serve brownies sprinkled with powdered sugar.

CHARLESTON CHEWS

Melissa A. Spatz
Atlanta, GA

Charleston Chews were passed down from my great-grandmother.

1 stick butter
1 cup honey graham cracker crumbs
1 package (6 ounces) semisweet chocolate chips
½ package (of 12-ounce package) butterscotch chips
1 package (7 ounces) coconut flakes
1 can (14 ounces) sweetened condensed milk
¾ cup pecans, chopped

Melt butter in 9x13-inch pan. Layer the following ingredients in order: graham cracker crumbs, chocolate chips, butterscotch chips, coconut flakes, condensed milk, and pecans. Bake at 350° for 35 minutes. **Makes 1 dozen.**

Serve bars with a cold glass of milk.

SCRUMPTIOUS SQUARES

Dorothy A. Carnes
Irving, TX

I was given this recipe when we lived in England in the early 1970s. It is guaranteed to be a smashing success each time it is served. Great for buffets or teas.

Shortbread:

¾ pound salted butter
¾ cup powdered sugar
3 cups sifted flour

Filling:

1½ cups margarine
1½ cups brown sugar
½ cup white KARO® corn syrup
1 can (14 ounces) sweetened condensed milk
1 tablespoon vanilla extract

Topping:

12 ounces to 1 pound CADBURY® chocolate
1 tablespoon margarine

Mix shortbread ingredients until crumbly. Chill before patting into pan. Press into 10½x16½-inch pan. Bake at 375° for 5 minutes, lower heat to 300° and continue baking 50 additional minutes. Should be light golden brown. Cool. Combine margarine, brown sugar, syrup and condensed milk over a low heat, stirring until dissolved. Bring to a boil, stirring constantly, then boil gently for 9 minutes; start counting when it is a full, rolling boil. Add vanilla, beat well, then pour onto shortbread. Cool. Melt chocolate and margarine in top of double boiler and spread over cooled caramelized filling. Chill and cut into 1½-inch squares.
Makes 20 squares.

Serve squares with chilled milk.

NANNY'S BAKED APPLES

If you want to light up your child's face and fill your home with a warm glow, try this recipe from my grandmother, Leona Wells Lampton. Nanny and my mother made this recipe for me when I was little. As I got older, they'd let me help, and I flipped! I loved helping. They also let me decide what to put in the apple's cavity—I felt like a pint-sized chef. Our fourteen-year-old son says the apples are *"fly"* (which means great!)

8 firm apples, washed and cored
1 tablespoon cinnamon
2 teaspoons nutmeg
1 cup water

Choice of fillings:

½ cup raisins
½ cup cranberry sauce
½ cup dates, chopped
½ cup dried mixed fruits
½ cup granola

Wash and core apples. Pare a thin section of skin from the top of each apple. Place apples close together in a baking dish and sprinkle with cinnamon and nutmeg. Fill the cavities of the apples with the filling of your choice, about one tablespoon of filling per apple. Add ½-inch of water and bake, basting with pan juices every 15 minutes. Cover and bake at 400° for 30 to 35 minutes. **Makes 8.**

Apples are done when they are easily pricked with a fork and still hold their shape.

Serve apples, warm or cold, topped with yogurt, cream or nondairy topping. Sprinkle cinnamon on top.

JAR BARS

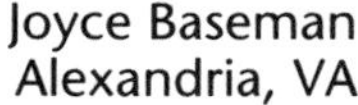

Joyce Baseman
Alexandria, VA

Every summer during my childhood I visited a favorite aunt who always fixed the foods I loved the most. Now, I try to be the special aunt and make these same oft-requested recipes for my own nieces and nephews. The recipes themselves are simple enough for them to do or at least help to make, which adds to the children's enjoyment as well.

2 eggs
½ cup vegetable oil
½ cup sugar
½ cup orange juice
1 cup flour
1½ teaspoons baking powder
½ teaspoon salt

Break eggs into a quart jar. Cover tightly. Shake ten times. Add oil and sugar. Shake 20 to 30 times. Add remaining ingredients. Cover and shake 40 times. Pour into greased 10x7- or 8x8-inch pan. Spread evenly. Bake at 375° for 20 minutes. Cut into squares when cool. **Serves 6.**

Bars can be iced with favorite frosting, and decorated with sprinkles.

APPLE CANDY PIE

Patty Campbell
Kenilworth, IL

I know there are many recipes for apple crisp; this is my mother's and is the best. My children want this instead of apple pie for Thanksgiving.

4 cups apples, sliced
1 cup brown sugar
½ cup water
¾ cup flour
½ cup butter
1 teaspoon cinnamon

Use a 9-inch glass pie plate. Place apple slices in pie plate. Sprinkle half of the sugar on top of the apples. Pour water over the sugar and apples. Place remaining ingredients in food processor. Pulse until crumbly. Sprinkle evenly over apples. Bake at 350° for 40 to 45 minutes. **Serves 8.**

Serve pie with cinnamon ice cream.

APRICOT FLAN PIE

Mrs. Ruth Ruder
Cincinnati, OH

I created this pie for a pie-baking contest and won Second Place. It's now a family favorite.

Flan:

3 tablespoons sugar
1 package (3 ounces) blanched almonds
1⅓ cups evaporated milk
¾ cup cream
3 eggs
3 egg yolks

Powdered Sugar Crust:

1 stick butter
½ cup sugar powdered sugar
1 cup flour

Apricot Glaze:

1 can (28 ounces) apricots, reserve juice
2 tablespoons sugar
½ teaspoon cornstarch
1 teaspoon almond extract

Flan: Heat sugar in a saucepan over low heat until melted and beginning to brown. Put in bottom of a 9- or 10-inch springform pan, tilting to coat pan. Let it cool. Toast almonds until lightly browned then process with blender or food processor until coarsely but evenly ground. Add evaporated milk, cream, eggs and egg yolks. Stir to mix, then blend on high until smooth.

Pour into springform pan lined with caramelized sugar. Bake at 325° for 45 minutes or until set. Cool and refrigerate overnight. The next day, invert onto pie crust (recipe follows below). Wipe any liquid sugar/syrup off with a paper towel or clean sponge.

Powdered Sugar Crust: Soften butter and mix with flour and sugar. Press into a 10-inch pie pan. Prick bottom with fork. Bake at 350° for 20 to 25 minutes or until slightly browned. Remove and cool.

Apricot Glaze: Reserve some juice from can, decorate top of flan with apricot halves in center and thin slices of apricot around edges, overlapping the slices like a deck of cards.

Puree remaining apricots, using enough to make 1½ cups of glaze in their juice. Add sugar, cornstarch and almond extract. Heat and stir until thick and immediately pour over top of apricots and entire pie, sealing to edges of crust. Cool in refrigerator until set. **Serves 8.**

FRESH BLUEBERRY PIE

Ellen Sherwood
Chesterfield, MO

I wanted something my husband and nephew could make together without much fuss or mess and that would be quick and easy. My young nephew had a great time baking, and he felt like he had accomplished something. When our families got together, my nephew was able to take credit for the dessert.

"I want to bake by myself. Can I have the recipe for the pie?"

¾ cup sugar
5 tablespoons cornstarch
4 cups fresh blueberries
1 teaspoon lemon peel, grated
2 (9-inch) prepared pie shells, unbaked
1 tablespoon margarine

Preheat oven to 425°. In large bowl, combine sugar and cornstarch. Add blueberries and lemon peel. Toss blueberries to coat well. Spoon blueberry mixture into a pie shell. Dot with margarine. Take the other pie shell out of its pie plate. Roll the pastry two inches larger than the pie plate. Make several slits to allow steam to escape. Cover pie with pastry. Seal and flute edge.

Bake in 425° oven for 35 to 45 minutes or until bubbly and crust is browned. **Serves 6 to 8.**

Serve pie with vanilla ice cream.

PEANUT BUTTER AND JELLY CHIFFON PIE

Dottie Haggerty
La Jolla, CA

This pie reminds my two sons and daughter of their favorite lunch box sandwich. They are now grown, (two M.D.s and a Ph.D.) and the memory lingers on and on and . . .

1 (9-inch) pie shell, baked
1 heaping cup creamy peanut butter
1 cup grape jelly
1 envelope gelatin
1 cup whipping cream, stiffly beaten
⅓ cup peanuts, finely chopped

Using a small rubber spatula, carefully line pie shell with peanut butter. Heat grape jelly and gelatin, stirring constantly over low heat, until gelatin is dissolved and mixture heated thoroughly. Cool, whisking until smooth. Stir into whipped cream. Pour into pie shell and sprinkle minced peanuts over top to garnish. Chill until firm, or freeze. **Serves 8.**

Serve pie with cold milk or hot coffee.

LEMON SURPRISE

Bonnie B. Swearingen
Chicago, IL

1 (9-inch) graham cracker crust
1 tablespoon butter, melted
1 can (14 ounces) sweetened condensed milk
4 egg yolks
½ cup fresh lemon juice
1 tablespoon fresh mint, chopped
4 egg whites, beaten
1 tablespoon powdered sugar

Before baking graham cracker crust, pour melted butter over crust, then bake in 350° oven for 3 to 5 minutes, just to brown the butter and seal the crust. Mix together milk, egg yolks, lemon juice and mint and pour into prepared pie crust. Beat egg whites and powdered sugar for meringue. Place meringue on top of pie mixture. Bake in 350° oven for 12 to 15 minutes or until browned. Let cool and refrigerate. **Serves 6 to 8.**

Serve pie garnished with fresh mint.

SOUR CREAM AND LEMON PIE

Susan Panish
Boston, MA

I have three daughters with very different tastes. We dubbed one *"the duty gourmet,"* another preferred peanut butter and jelly to real food and the third mostly preferred macaroni . . . but they all loved this pie. They are now grown up . . . one with a son of her own, and as soon as he gets off mother's milk, he too will try the Sour Cream and Lemon Pie.

1 cup sugar
3 tablespoons cornstarch
¼ cup butter
¼ cup lemon juice
3 egg yolks
1 lemon zest, grated
1 cup milk
1 cup sour cream
1 (9-inch) pie shell, baked
¼ cup heavy cream, whipped

Combine sugar, cornstarch, butter, lemon juice, egg yolks, lemon zest and milk. Cook over medium heat, stirring constantly until thickened and smooth. Chill.

Fold the sour cream into the chilled lemon mixture and spoon into baked pie shell. Chill well. Serve topped with whipped cream. **Serves 6 to 8.**

Serve pie with tall glasses of mint tea.

GRANDMA'S BANANA PUDDING

Amy Severs
Rowlett, TX

My grandmother taught me how to make this family favorite when I was a little girl, and I'm still making it today.

1 cup sugar
5 level tablespoons flour
2 cups milk
4 egg yolks
1 tablespoon vanilla extract
2 bananas, sliced
2 cups vanilla wafers

Mix sugar and flour together, add ½ cup milk and stir. Beat in egg yolks by hand. Add remaining milk and cook over low heat until thickened. Remove from heat. Stir in vanilla. Pour into a bowl lined with vanilla wafers and banana slices. Chill. **Serves 4 to 6.**

Serve pudding with hot tea or cold milk.

BREAD PUDDING

Taryn M. Valle
Newton Center, MA

I think this was my grandmother's recipe, but it's been copied over so many times. . . I'm not sure. My three-year-old considers it a fine reward for a clean plate.

1 cup brown sugar, packed
4 slices bread, buttered
2⅓ cups milk
2 eggs
1 teaspoon vanilla extract
½ teaspoon nutmeg
½ teaspoon cinnamon

Spread brown sugar over bottom of buttered baking dish; tear buttered bread and place on top of sugar. Beat milk, eggs and vanilla and pour over all. Sprinkle the nutmeg and cinnamon over the top. Bake at 350° for 1 hour or until moderately brown and puffed to top of dish. Add raisins and nuts if you like.
Serves 6 to 8.

Serve pudding with brandy-flavored whipped cream (fold 1 teaspoon of brandy flavoring into 2 cups of whipped cream).

NOODLE PUDDING

Brunice (Mrs. John) Breiner
New York, NY

- 1 package (8 ounces) broad noodles
- 1 carton (8 ounces) creamed cottage cheese
- ¼ cup margarine, melted
- ½ cup sour cream
- 2 eggs, beaten
- ½ cup sugar
- 1 orange, zest (only) grated before peeling
- 2 apples, grated
- 1 can (8 ounces) crushed pineapple, drained
- 1 cup white raisins

Cook noodles, rinse and drain. Mix all ingredients together. Generously grease a baking dish and heat dish before adding mixture. Sprinkle with cinnamon and bake in 350° oven for 50 minutes. **Serves 8 to 10.**

Serve pudding with whipped cream sprinkled with nutmeg.

RICE PUDDING

Elton John
London, England

Elton John's favorite dessert.

- 4 cups water
- 2 cups rice
- 1 stick cinnamon
- 2 cups sugar
- ½ teaspoon salt
- ½ gallon milk
- 2 tablespoons ground cinnamon
- 1 cup raisins

Mix water, rice and stick cinnamon. Let this mixture stand for about an hour; rice will then be tender. Cook the mixture over low heat for 25 minutes. When the rice is cooked, add sugar, salt and milk. Continue cooking for another 40 minutes, until rice gets sticky. Pour rice into a baking dish. Stir in ground cinnamon and raisins. Bake at 375° for 25 minutes. **Serves 10.**

Serve topped with whipped cream sprinkled with cinnamon.

KIDS' KOBBLER

Deborah (Debbie) Thomas
Dallas, TX

Kids can measure out the easy ingredients and stir the batter. I learned this recipe as a child from my grandmother who taught me that cooking is a way to share love.

1 stick butter or margarine
1 cup flour
1 cup sugar
1 teaspoon baking powder
1 cup milk
1 teaspoon vanilla extract
2 cans (1 pound each) sweetened fruit, drained (sliced peaches, apricots, berries or cherries)
Ground cinnamon, if desired

Preheat oven to 350°. Put butter in 2-quart deep casserole or baking dish and melt in oven. Combine flour, sugar, baking powder, milk and vanilla. Blend lightly; batter will be slightly lumpy. Pour into center of melted butter. Top with fruit and whatever juices remain in can after draining. Do not stir. Sprinkle with cinnamon, if desired. Bake at 350° for 1 hour. Sweetened fresh or thawed frozen fruits may be substituted. **Serves 6 to 8.**

Serve cobbler warm with a scoop of vanilla ice cream.

PEACH COBBLER

Mary Ann Mobley Collins
Beverly Hills, CA

When visiting friends in my home state of Mississippi, I mentioned how much I love peach cobbler and they immediately made me this peach cobbler (it is a very fast recipe). I have clung onto this for dear life as it is the best I have ever tasted.

"Yum! Yum!"

6 to 8 large, very ripe peaches, peeled, seeded and sliced
1 cup sugar
1 stick butter
1 cup flour
1 cup sugar
1 cup milk
Vanilla ice cream (optional)

If you are using fresh peaches, seed, peel and slice into thin slices. Put sliced peaches in plastic bowl and pour 1 cup of sugar over the sliced peaches. Stir well. Cover tightly and place in refrigerator for 2 hours. Place 1 stick of butter in bottom of a rectangular baking dish and place in oven at 400° until butter melts. In separate bowl, mix flour, 1 cup sugar and milk, beating well with a whisk. Pour mixture over melted butter, don't mix. Spoon peaches over batter mixture. VERY IMPORTANT: DO NOT STIR PEACHES INTO BATTER. Bake at 400° for 40 minutes or until top becomes golden brown. (The mixture comes up around the peaches and turns golden brown.) **Serves 10 to 12.**

Note: Can be made with 1 can (20 ounces) cling peaches, sliced. If you are using canned peaches, add only a small amount of juice from the can. Also, do not soak canned peaches in the first cup of sugar. The second cup of sugar is still needed for the batter.

Serve cobbler hot with vanilla ice cream.

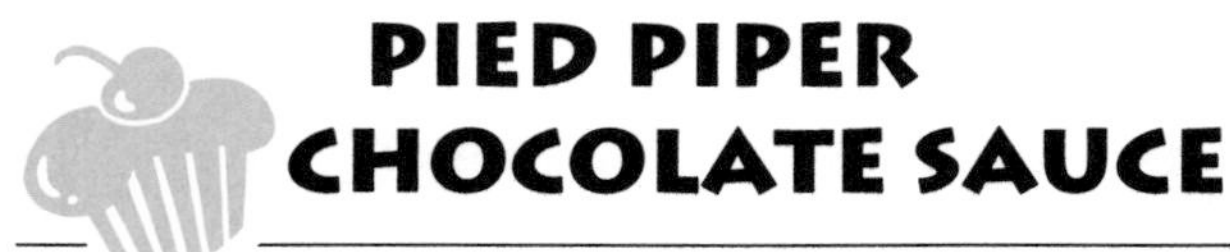

PIED PIPER CHOCOLATE SAUCE

Mrs. Joe S. Thompson
Sherman, TX

My chocolate sauce is an old family hand-me-down. When my daughters' noses were out of joint and I cooked this sauce—the aroma brought them down to the kitchen with smiles.

2 tablespoons margarine
1 square bitter chocolate
⅓ cup milk
1 cup sugar
1 teaspoon vanilla extract

Melt margarine and chocolate. Add milk, let come to a boil and boil for 1 minute. Add sugar, stir and bring to a boil, boiling for 3 minutes. Remove from medium heat, add vanilla. Refrigerate leftovers. Add a drop or two of milk to reheat. **Serves 2.**

Wonderful on ice cream or anything.

TAFFY APPLE SALAD

Barbara G. Levin
Winnetka, IL

"I could eat the whole bowl—it tastes just like taffy apples."

½ cup sugar
1 tablespoon cornstarch
2 tablespoons lemon juice
1 egg, beaten
1 carton (8 ounces) whipped topping
1 can (20 ounces) pineapple tidbits, drained, reserving liquid
4 apples, unpeeled, cored and cut into small pieces
2½ cups miniature marshmallows
½ cup salted peanuts

In a medium saucepan, combine sugar, cornstarch, lemon juice, egg and pineapple juice. Cook until it boils and thickens, stirring continuously, about 10 minutes. Allow to cool. In a large bowl, combine whipped topping and cooled mixture. Stir in pineapple, apples, marshmallows and peanuts just before serving. **Serves 4 to 6.**

GRANDMA'S APPLE BUTTER

Sue Zelickson
Minneapolis, MN

Delicious on toast or warmed and served on vanilla ice cream.

24 apples, peeled and cored
3 cups cider
2 cups packed brown sugar
1 cup granulated sugar
1½ teaspoons cinnamon
¾ teaspoon cloves
¼ teaspoon nutmeg
¼ teaspoon allspice
¼ teaspoon salt
1 lemon, grated zest

Peel and core apples. Cook with cider over medium heat until apples are soft, stirring occasionally. Put through a food mill or press through a colander and measure 11 cups of sieved fruit. Combine with remaining ingredients in a large ovenproof casserole or kettle. Bake, uncovered, at 325° until thick, about 2 to 2½ hours. Stir every 30 to 40 minutes. Spoon into hot, sterilized jars, seal and cool to room temperature, then refrigerate.
Makes 4 to 5 pints.

Note: Preferred apple varieties are McIntosh, Lakeland and Haralson.

HULA HOOPS

Allan H. Fradkin, M.D.
Galveston, TX

Kids will love the name as well as these sweet nut treats.

Cookie Crust:

½ cup butter, softened
¼ cup sugar
1 cup flour, sifted

Frosting:

2 tablespoons butter, softened
1¼ cups powdered sugar
1 tablespoon milk
½ cup coconut, toasted

Nut Filling:

2 eggs, beaten
½ cup coconut
1½ cups light brown sugar
1 jar (3½ ounces) macadamia nuts, chopped
2 tablespoons vanilla extract
½ teaspoon salt
¼ teaspoon baking powder

Cream butter and sugar. Work in flour until smoothly blended. Pat ingredients into the bottom of 9x9-inch pan. Bake at 350° for 18 minutes or until golden. For the filling, beat eggs slightly. Add coconut, brown sugar, macadamia nuts, vanilla, salt and baking powder. Stir until well-blended. Spread filling over crust. Bake in a 350° oven for 25 minutes, or until browned and firm to the touch. Let cool in pan.

For the frosting, beat butter, sugar and milk until smooth. Spread evenly over filling. Garnish with toasted coconut as desired. Cut into one-inch squares. **Serves 8 to 10.**

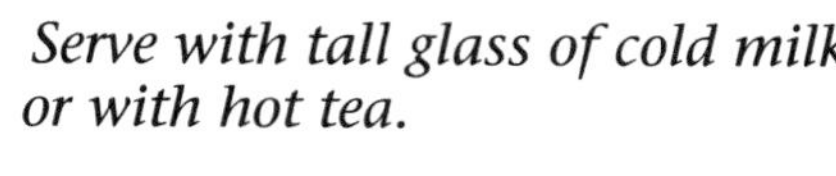

Serve with tall glass of cold milk or with hot tea.

CHAPTER SIX

WHERE HAVE ALL THE PICNICS GONE?

Like convertibles and drive-in movies, they almost disappeared with the invention of central air-conditioning. But, if convertibles can make a comeback, so can picnics. (We can't promise drive-ins.) It should come as no surprise that as outdoorsy as InCirclers seem to be, picnics out are *in*, regardless of weather. And, if kids can scarf up greasy burgers taken to the park, imagine their reaction to something really good from home like Chicken Quesadillas or Walking Salad? After all, it takes just two things to make a successful picnic: one, transportable food whether it's in a brown bag or a fancy English basket; and two, kids and grown-ups to enjoy every morsel, leaving nothing behind for the ants.

BEST CHICKEN SALAD

Bobbie Davis
New Rochelle, NY

As a program director for Girl Scouts® of America, I was experimenting with low-fat recipes for the girls to make as part of the patch program called *"Looking Good, Feeling Good."*

½ cup yogurt
3 tablespoons low-fat mayonnaise
2 tablespoons honey mustard
3 medium-sized kosher dill pickles, chopped
3 stalks celery, chopped
4 chicken breasts, cooked and cubed

Mix together all ingredients and enjoy! **Serves 4.**

Serve salad with toasted wheat bread.

BOW TIE SALAD

Kay (Nina) Peeples
Houston, TX

Dressing:
1¼ cups mayonnaise
⅓ cup Parmesan cheese, grated
⅓ cup fresh parsley, chopped
¼ teaspoon oregano
¼ teaspoon basil
1 small garlic clove, minced

Salad:
4 ounces bow tie pasta, cooked and drained
4 ounces ham, cut into ½-inch cubes
1 can (8½ ounces) artichoke hearts, drained and quartered
1 cup broccoli flowerets
½ cup combined red, green and yellow bell pepper, chopped
1 cup mushrooms, sliced
1 cup zucchini, thinly sliced

Dressing: In a bowl, stir ingredients until smoothly blended.

Salad: Add pasta and all salad ingredients to bowl with the dressing. Toss well and coat thoroughly. Cover and refrigerate for 2 hours to let the flavors blend. **Serves 6.**

Serve salad with bagel chips.

CURRIED TURKEY SALAD

Daniel Bifano
Santa Barbara, CA

Both my parents were born in Italy, and I have a big family on both sides. This recipe was given to me by my mother, who got it from her mother-in-law.

1½ cups mayonnaise
1 cup plain yogurt
2 tablespoons butter, softened
2 tablespoons curry powder
½ cup CROSSE & BLACKWELL® Major Grey's chutney, minced
4 pounds turkey breast, cooked and torn into small pieces
2 cups celery, chopped
1 cup scallions, chopped
2 cups seedless red grapes, sliced

In a large ceramic bowl, mix mayonnaise, yogurt, butter, curry powder and chutney. Add turkey, celery, scallions and grapes. Mix well. **Serves 12.**

Garnish salad with lightly toasted unsalted cashews or seedless red grapes. Serve salad with cantaloupe or honeydew on the side.

MACARONI SALAD

Robin Hahn
San Jose, CA

"Best macaroni salad I ever ate, plus it's easy enough for me to make." Matthew (age 12).

1 package (12 ounces) macaroni, cooked and drained
1 cup gherkin pickles, chopped
1 can (6 ounces) medium-sized olives, pitted and chopped
1 small red onion, chopped
1 medium tomato, chopped
1 can (4½ ounces) whole medium-sized shrimp
¾ cup mayonnaise
Salt, pepper, and paprika

Cook macaroni, drain. Rinse with cold water to cool; drain again. Add pickles, olives, onion, tomatoes, shrimp and mayonnaise to the cooked macaroni; toss well. Add salt, pepper and paprika to taste. Chill overnight before serving. **Serves 6 to 8.**

Serve salad on bed of crisp lettuce with sourdough bread.

NOODLE SALAD

Angela Jhin
Tiburon, CA

When I studied in England, my guardian, who was Chinese, always served this.

Salad:
- **¾ pound egg noodles**
- **1 tablespoon sesame oil**
- **3 eggs**
- **1 cup cooked ham, shredded**
- **½ cup cooked chicken, shredded**
- **½ cup celery, grated**
- **½ cup cucumber, grated**
- **½ cup carrots, grated**

Dressing:
- **2 teaspoons sesame oil**
- **1 tablespoon sesame paste**
- **½ teaspoon salt**
- **2 tablespoons soy sauce**
- **2 teaspoons vinegar**
- **2 cups chicken broth**

Cook noodles and drain. Mix with 1 tablespoon sesame oil and chill in refrigerator. Beat eggs, fry in pan and chop. Arrange eggs, meat and vegetables on top of noodles. Pour on salad dressing when ready to serve. Mix all ingredients thoroughly. **Serves 6 to 8.**

Serve salad with fresh fruit and sesame crackers.

WALKING SALAD

Courtney H. Scott
Spartanburg, SC

For years this has been our family's *"one piece picnic."* A healthy snack, Walking Salad is great indoors on a rainy day picnic too. Eat while you are on the move!

"Dining room tables don't need chairs."

- **1 apple, cored**
- **2 tablespoons peanut butter**
- **1 teaspoon raisins**

Core a red or green apple. Mix the raisins and peanut butter and stuff hollowed core of apple with the mixture. **Serves 1.**

Serve salad with juice of choice.

DEVILED EGGS WITH FRANKFURTERS

Beverly Davydiuk
Bedford, TX

My husband and I often took the grandchildren fishing and picnicking. Whenever we picked them up for a fishing adventure, their first question was, *"Did you bring the deviled eggs and the fishing poles?"*

6 large eggs, hard-cooked
2 tablespoons mayonnaise
1 tablespoon prepared mustard
⅛ teaspoon curry powder
¼ teaspoon salt
½ teaspoon Worcestershire sauce
⅓ cup frankfurters, finely chopped
Black pepper, freshly ground
Paprika

Crack and peel eggs; cut crosswise in half. Remove yolks and mash with mayonnaise, mustard, curry, salt and Worcestershire sauce. Add chopped frankfurter and stuff mixture into egg white halves. Sprinkle pepper and paprika over eggs. **Serves 12.**

Serve eggs with Friend's Meatloaf on page 103.

TURKEY-BERRY SANDWICHES

Susan Douglas
Topeka, KS

This is a family favorite for using up Thanksgiving leftovers. We often wrap them up and take them for *"tailgating"* at local football games. They travel very well!

2 cups cream cheese, softened
1 cup crushed cranberry sauce
¼ cup almonds, slivered
1 tablespoon orange peel, grated
5 buns or croissants
3 cups sprouts or lettuce, shredded
1½ pounds smoked or leftover turkey

Blend cream cheese, cranberry sauce, almonds and orange peel. Split buns or croissants in half and spread mixture on one side. Add sprouts or lettuce and top with turkey and other half of bun or croissant. **Serves 5.**

Serve sandwiches with spicy potato chips.

CHICKEN QUESADILLAS

Billy O'Connor, Jr.
Dallas, TX

I have children ages four, seven and ten who love this recipe. For them I make it on the mild side; other times I really spice it up. The recipe came from a good friend who is a professional chef.

4 tablespoons cooking oil
2 flour tortillas
¼ cup chicken, cooked and cubed
3 tablespoons Monterey Jack cheese, grated
3 tablespoons Cheddar cheese, grated
2 tablespoons salsa

Heat oil in 10-inch sauté pan. Lay tortilla flat in the pan and sprinkle with remaining ingredients. Top with a second tortilla and fry at medium heat for 2½ minutes on each side. Cut in quarters. **Serves 1.**

Serve with dollops of sour cream and salsa and sprinkle with cilantro.

SPINACH BALLS

Linda Svehlak
Dallas, TX

A sorority sister of mine gave me this recipe which had been a favorite in her family for years.

2 packages (10 ounces each) chopped frozen spinach, thawed and drained
½ large onion, finely chopped
6 eggs, well beaten
¾ cup butter, melted
½ cup Parmesan cheese, grated
½ tablespoon pepper
1½ teaspoons garlic salt
½ teaspoon thyme
3 cups PEPPERIDGE FARM® herb-seasoned stuffing

Combine all ingredients and mix thoroughly. Shape into small balls and place on cookie sheets. Bake at 325° for 15 minutes. **Makes 40 balls.**

Dip spinach balls into favorite onion dip.

BBQ BEEF BRISKET

Kathy Scott
Atlanta, GA

The first time I tasted the BBQ Beef Brisket was at a tailgate party for a football game. From that time on, our boys (teenagers at the time) wanted *"that stringy beef."* I've been preparing it for years now because of its convenience to our roaming life style. We have a cabin in the mountains, so I prepare it, divide it into portions and put it in small sealable, plastic bags and freeze. It's easy to reheat and place on a toasted piece of French bread or bun. This recipe has seen many Monday night football games in front of a fireplace, after school snacks—and winter lunches, plus Fourth of July picnics.

1 brisket (3 pounds)
½ package dry onion soup mix
1 cup barbecue sauce
½ cup sweet and sour sauce
French bread

Place brisket on heavy-duty foil and sprinkle with onion soup mix. Seal foil and bake at 300° for 2½ hours. Do not open. Refrigerate overnight. Unwrap and scrape off fat and onion mix. Thinly slice against the grain. Mix barbecue sauce with sweet and sour sauce. Pour sauce over beef, letting it ooze down between slices. Refold foil and seal well. Heat at 200° for 2 hours. Or, divide into portions and keep in freezer. Reheat in foil or covered dish.
Serves 8 to 10.

Serve brisket with fresh French bread.

TASTE OF SUMMER RIBS

Gay Curtiss-Lusher
Denver, CO

This is a frequent summer treat, and a real family project. I shop for the ribs and marinate them; my husband finishes them on the grill. But, the real secret is in the precooking in the oven.

Ribs:

- **4 pounds beef baby back ribs**
- **1 lemon, sliced**
- **1 onion, sliced**
- **Salt and pepper, freshly ground, to taste**
- **1 to 1½ cups favorite barbecue sauce**

Denver Barbecue Sauce:

- **4 cups ketchup**
- **1 bottle chili sauce**
- **¾ cup brown sugar, packed**
- **½ teaspoon cayenne pepper**
- **1 teaspoon pepper, freshly ground**
- **1½ teaspoons salt**
- **1 cup cider vinegar**
- **1 tablespoon Dijon mustard**
- **1 tablespoon Worcestershire sauce**

Ribs: Preheat oven to 325°. In a large roasting pan, place ribs on a rack in a single layer. Place sliced lemon and onion on top and season with salt and pepper. Add ¼-inch water, in bottom of pan, cover, and bake for 1 hour. Remove ribs from the pan and discard the water, lemon and onion. At this point, the ribs may be finished in the oven or on the grill. Place ribs on a baking sheet or on the grill. Brush ¾ cup sauce on ribs and bake at 350° or grill for 10 to 15 minutes. Turn ribs over, brush with remaining sauce and bake or grill for 10 minutes more.

Denver Barbecue Sauce: Combine all ingredients in a large saucepan and mix well. Simmer over low heat, stirring frequently, for 30 minutes. Remove from heat and cool. Store in a glass container. **Serves 8.**

Serve ribs with grilled corn (in the husk) and baked beans.

GRILLED MARINATED VEGETABLES

Marianne P. Hinrichs
Corona del Mar, CA

Everyone loves this! And it's an easy way to get the children to eat more veggies. We've been serving it with success to all age groups for a few years, and it seems to go well with any entrée.

2 Japanese eggplants, halved lengthwise

6 whole green onions, trimmed

3 peppers, red, yellow and green, quartered and seeded

2 tablespoons balsamic vinegar

½ teaspoon Dijon mustard

6 tablespoons olive oil

1 tablespoon fresh oregano and thyme, minced

Salt and pepper to taste

Arrange vegetables in a 9x13-inch glass dish. Mix vinegar and mustard in a small bowl and whisk in oil in a thin stream. Mix in herbs, salt and pepper. Pour over veggies. Marinate 2 hours.

Prepare barbecue grill. Place eggplants, skin side down on grill for 3 minutes; turn eggplant, add green onions and grill 5 more minutes. Remove eggplant and onions and keep warm. Arrange peppers on greased rack, skin side down. Grill 5 minutes. Brush with marinade during cooking time. **Serves 4.**

Serve vegetables with grilled chicken breasts.

STUFFED CHEESE PIE

Betty (Mrs. Eddie) Williams
Arlington, TX

2 boxes (1 pound each) KRAFT VELVEETA® cheese, room temperature
1 package (8 ounces) cream cheese, room temperature
1 pound bacon, cooked until crisp and crumbled
1 can (7 ounces) chopped green chilies, drained
1 can (4¼ ounces) chopped black olives
2 tomatoes, finely chopped
6 green onions, chop entire onion

Divide each box of cheese into four equal parts. Lay each part on a piece of plastic wrap and press with hands to flatten. Cover with another piece of plastic wrap and roll thin. Place in a pie pan with plastic wrap on bottom, remove top plastic wrap and spread with cream cheese. Layer bacon, chilies, olives, tomatoes and onions. Remove the top plastic wrap from the remaining cheese and place over layered ingredients. Remove plastic wrap and press edges together and trim as you would a pie. Cover with a large serving plate and invert, remove plastic wrap. I like to decorate the top with the excess cheese. Example: form chilies and roll in red pepper and use cilantro for leaves.
Serves 10 to 12.

Serve with crackers and blue corn chips.

BARRY'S CHEESE DIP

Caryn Kay
Glencoe, IL

My husband Barry has been making this for years, and his sons have always loved it. Now that they are grown, they still expect to have it whenever they drop by.

"Where's Dad's dip?"

2 packages (8 ounces each) cream cheese
⅓ cup half-and-half
2 cloves garlic, pressed
1 to 2 teaspoons of TABASCO® sauce
1 teaspoon fresh lemon juice
2½ tablespoons celery seed
1 small onion, grated

Soften the cream cheese and gradually add the cream until the mixture is creamy. Add the rest of the ingredients and blend together with a fork. Refrigerate until ready to serve.

Serve dip with chips, carrot sticks or other raw vegetables.

GORGONZOLA CHEESE SPREAD

Karen Merz
Atlanta, GA

I enjoyed something very similar to this about ten years ago in an Atlanta restaurant that is now out of business. My husband and I were dating then; I've made it frequently ever since, and our six-year-old son and twenty-month-old daughter like it as well.

8 ounces Gorgonzola, Italian or domestic, softened
12 ounces cream cheese, softened

In a food processor, blend together the cheeses until smooth and creamy. Spoon into small crock and refrigerate several hours until firm. **Serves 6.**

Hint: Blending by hand does not result in smooth consistency; food processor is a must.

Serve dip with French bread or crackers.

GRANDMA'S MUSH-MUSH

Nancy
(Mrs. Donald C.) Thomas
Indian Wells, CA

My grandchildren named this recipe when our basset hound knocked one of the dishes to the kitchen floor and scattered the food all over. The children shouted, *"Look at Grandma's mush-mush,"* and the name stuck.

1½ pounds ground beef, lean
1 large onion, chopped
2 tablespoons olive oil
1 can (28 ounces) peeled whole tomatoes, undrained
1 package (16 ounces) small elbow macaroni
Salt and pepper, to taste

Brown the ground beef and chopped onion in olive oil. Drain fat juices. Place meat and onion mixture into 1-quart casserole dish. Add whole tomatoes and liquid to meat mixture. Cook elbow noodles according to package directions, rinse and add to casserole dish. Mix all ingredients together. Add salt and pepper to taste. Bake covered at 350° for 1 hour. **Serves 6.**

Serve with a salad of crisp green lettuce, mandarin oranges, a poppy-seed dressing and crusty bread.

BLUEBERRY GINGERBREAD

Laura Wertheimer
Washington, DC

We vacation in August on Martha's Vineyard and have spent many mornings picking wild blueberries. After many rounds of jam, pies and tarts, we hit upon gingerbread as the perfect use for our many blueberries and the perfect dessert for our afternoon beach picnics.

½ cup boiling water
½ cup dark molasses
1 tablespoon honey
1 teaspoon baking soda
5 tablespoons sweet butter, softened
1 cup light brown sugar, firmly packed
1 large egg
¼ cup solid packed pumpkin (not pumpkin pie filling)
2 teaspoons ground ginger
1 teaspoon cinnamon
2 cups flour
1 tablespoon baking powder
1½ cups wild blueberries or 1 cup big blueberries

Preheat the oven to 350°. Spray the bottom and sides of a 9x13-inch pan with cooking spray and set aside. Boil water; add molasses, honey and baking soda, set aside to cool until lukewarm. Combine the butter and sugar and beat at medium-high speed for 4 minutes, until light and fluffy. Add the egg and pumpkin and mix thoroughly. Sift together the ginger, cinnamon, flour and baking powder. Fold half of the dry ingredients into the butter and sugar mixture and beat until combined. Stir in all of the molasses mixture. Add the remaining dry ingredients and blend thoroughly. With a spatula, gently fold the blueberries into the gingerbread batter. Put the batter into the prepared pan. Bake for 30 minutes, or until a wooden toothpick inserted in the middle comes out clean. Place the gingerbread pan on a cooling rack until cool and cut into squares. **Serves 8 to 10.**

Serve gingerbread with whipped cream.

MOWRY'S SOFT SUGAR COOKIES

Diane Eberly
Plano, TX

This recipe was given to my mother from a neighbor, Mary Mowry, in Topeka, Kansas, and we have both been using it ever since. These are the most wonderful, soft sugar cookies around. Kids of all ages go crazy for these cookies, and they disappear quickly.

¾ cup shortening
1 stick margarine
2 cups sugar
3 teaspoons vanilla extract
3 large or 4 small eggs
2 cups flour
½ teaspoon salt
6 teaspoons baking powder
3 cups flour
⅔ cup orange juice

Cream together shortening, margarine and sugar. Mix until smooth and creamy. Add eggs one at a time and beat well. Add vanilla. Sift 2 cups flour with salt and baking powder. Add 3 cups flour alternately with orange juice. This makes a stiff dough. Drop by spoonfuls onto ungreased cookie sheet. Spread out each drop with back of spoon. Sprinkle with granulated sugar. Bake in a 425° oven for 10 minutes or until lightly browned. **Makes 4 to 5 dozen.**

CHOCOLATE OATMEAL COOKIES

Sherrie Reddick
Wichita Falls, TX

This recipe was my late grandmother's recipe which I always helped to make. Now I make them with my granddaughter and it's a nice way to remember my grandmother, year after year.

1 cup brown sugar
1 cup granulated sugar
¾ cup butter
2 eggs
½ cup sour cream
2 cups oatmeal
½ teaspoon salt
1 teaspoon cinnamon
1 teaspoon soda
1¾ cups flour
1 cup raisins, ground
¼ cup cocoa

Cream sugars and butter. Add eggs and sour cream, mixing well. Add oatmeal, salt, cinnamon, soda, flour, raisins and cocoa. Mix well. Drop by rounded teaspoons on greased cookie sheets. Bake at 350° for 8 to 10 minutes. **Makes 3 dozen.**

WATERMELON SHERBERT

Mrs. Alfred W. Lasher, Jr.
Houston, TX

This has been a family favorite for warm weather dinners, barbecues and the Fourth of July.

"Mom, let's have this again soon!"

2 cups CARNATION® instant nonfat dry milk
1 cup whole milk
½ cup cold water
2 envelopes gelatin
¾ cup sugar
2 cups ripe watermelon, pureed
1 small bunch mint
Red food coloring

Stir dry milk crystals into whole milk. In cold water, soften sugar and gelatin and pour into milk mixture. Cook over low heat, stirring constantly until gelatin and sugar have dissolved. Cool. Pureé enough watermelon pulp in electric blender to make 2 cups. Stir into cooled milk mixture and add enough food coloring to make a pretty pink color. Put in refrigerator tray or mold. When firm, unmold and serve in molded form, individual dishes, or in a carved watermelon basket. Garnish with watermelon balls and mint leaves. **Serves 10 to 12.**

Serve sherbert with crisp shortbread cookies.

OLD-FASHIONED ICE CREAM

Neiman Marcus
CLASSIC

Old-Fashioned Ice Cream will make you remember picnics of your childhood.

½ cup sugar
⅛ teaspoon salt
6 egg yolks, lightly beaten
2 cups milk, scalded
2 cups evaporated milk
1 tablespoon vanilla

Mix sugar, salt and egg yolks thoroughly. Add milk slowly and cook in top of a double boiler, stirring until mixture coats a spoon. Cool and strain. Add evaporated milk and vanilla. Pour into an ice cream freezer and freeze, according to freezer directions. If using an ice-packed freezer, use 8 parts ice to 1 part salt. **Makes 1½ quarts.**

CHAPTER SEVEN

HOME IS WHERE THE HOLIDAYS ARE

Find the table leaf, break out the good crystal, china and silver. For minutes the board groans, then, when it's all over, the guests groan with pleasure. Competition among the family's best cooks flourishes. Is the new bride's dressing on a par with Aunt Catherine's? InCirclers are all over the lot when it comes to holiday cooking. Some keep to the tried-and-true; others are more adventuresome, so we've included recipes for both genres. As you scan this chapter, just pretend you're at a neighborhood recipe exchange party and you'll be sure to come home with something wonderful to add to your own repertoire.

SURPRISE GARDEN DESSERT

Dr. Roberta H. Markman
Huntington Beach, CA

My mother always made these for children's birthdays and brought them in on a tray to the table. I can remember thinking that all the flowers were smiling at the birthday boy or girl. And we all loved to pretend we were eating dirt!

"My mom won't spank me for eating this dirt; it's awesome! It's the funnest dessert I ever had."

8 clay flower pots, 3 inches in diameter
1 half-gallon of ice cream, chocolate or vanilla
8 flowers on stick or wire supports or in straws
1 bar (2 pounds) sweet cooking chocolate, shaved
1 piece of aluminum foil

Boil eight clay flower pots in a large vessel to sterilize. Cut small circles of aluminum foil to cover the bottoms of the pots so that the hole is covered. Fill the pots with either chocolate or vanilla ice cream and place pots in the freezer. Just before serving, remove pots from freezer and cover the ice cream with the shaved chocolate to resemble "dirt." Cover the bottom part of each flower stem with foil and insert each flower in the center of each pot so that the foil-covered part of the stem does not show. Then convince each child that it's OK to eat it! **Serves 8.**

Serve with chocolate cookies.

CHOCOLATE PIES

Susan Roberds
Dallas, TX

When I was a young girl, on my birthday, instead of cake, I always requested that my mother make this chocolate pie.

1 quart milk
½ cup butter
1½ squares chocolate
2½ cups sugar
2 teaspoons salt
1 cup flour
3 eggs
1 can (12 ounces) evaporated milk
2 teaspoons vanilla extract
3 (9-inch) pie crusts, baked
2½ cups heavy cream
Grated chocolate, for garnish

In a double boiler, combine milk, butter and chocolate until very hot, but not boiling. In bowl, mix sugar, salt and flour. Add eggs and evaporated milk and vanilla. Beat until well mixed. When chocolate-butter mixture is melted, remove ¼ cup and stir into egg mixture. Then combine the sugar-egg mixture with chocolate. Cook for 20 minutes, stirring constantly. Let cool. Fill baked pie crusts. Top with whipped cream and grated chocolate. Keep refrigerated. **Makes three 9-inch pies.**

Serve pie with mint tea.

VALENTINE COOKIES

B. Rhoads Fearn
San Franicsco, CA

When I was in grade school, my mother made heart-shaped cookies with my classmates' names on them every Valentine's Day—plus a heart-shaped cake for the teachers' lounge. Of course, she only had two children and there were only twenty-plus students in each class.

By the time I had one child each in kindergarten, second, fourth, sixth and eighth grades I was making 167 cookies and three cakes. My fingers would be numb from writing names, and I would stagger into bed about 1:30 a.m. However, my heart is warmed watching my daughter doing the same.

⅔ cup butter
¾ cup sugar
1 egg
1 teaspoon vanilla extract
2 cups flour, sifted
1½ teaspoons baking powder
¼ teaspoon salt

Thoroughly cream butter and sugar, add egg and beat until fluffy. Add vanilla. Sift dry ingredients and stir into creamed mixture. Divide dough into two balls and wrap in plastic. Refrigerate at least 1 hour or up to 24 hours. Roll out one batch at a time to ⅛-inch on a floured board and cut into appropriate shapes. Bake at 375° for 12 minutes. **Makes 2 dozen.**

Serve cookies with flavored hot tea.

BEST SUGAR COOKIE

Jayne Gross
Naperville, IL

All of my friends, young and old, like these cookies. These will bring raves for Valentine's Day, Easter, Fourth of July, Halloween, Thanksgiving and Christmas.

Cookies:

1 cup butter
¾ cup oil
¾ cup sugar
1 cup powdered sugar
2 eggs
2 teaspoons vanilla extract
4½ cups flour
1 teaspoon soda
½ teaspoon salt
1 teaspoon cream of tartar

Powdered Sugar Icing:

2 tablespoons butter, softened
4 cups powdered sugar, sifted
½ to ⅔ cup milk
½ teaspoon vanilla extract
½ teaspoon almond extract

Cookies: Beat butter and oil together. Gradually add sugars, beating well. Add eggs and vanilla. Mix well. Combine flour, soda, salt and cream of tartar. Gradually add to butter mixture and mix well. Refrigerate for several hours. Roll out gently on lightly floured surface with lightly floured rolling pin to about ¼-inch thickness. Use any type of cookie cutter. Bake at 375° for 10 minutes or until edges are barely brown. Don't overbake. This entire recipe can be done by hand or with a mixer. **Makes 3 dozen.**

Powdered Sugar Icing: Mix softened butter into 1 cup of the sugar, gradually add milk, then add vanilla and almond extracts. Continue adding sugar and milk until you reach the consistency you desire. Icing should be fairly thin. Add food coloring to icing and decorate as you wish.

Note: Can also use clean pillowcase, dusted PLENTIFULLY with flour for rolling surface.

Serve cookies with hot chocolate milk.

BLUEBERRY COFFEE CAKE

Julie Ansfield
Milwaukee, WI

This is a favorite of my son and my stepson. Both seem to show up in the kitchen at the same time to make certain the portions are equal. I always make this on July third, so we can return home from an early Declaration Day parade and have a patriotic breakfast.

Coffee Cake:

¼ cup butter
¾ cup sugar
1 egg
2 cups flour
2 teaspoons baking powder
½ teaspoon salt
½ cup milk
2 cups blueberries

Topping:

½ cup sugar
½ teaspoon cinnamon
1 teaspoon water
⅓ cup flour
¼ cup butter

Coffee Cake: Cream butter and sugar together. Add egg. Mix together dry ingredients. Add dry mixture in three portions, alternating with milk. Fold in blueberries.

Topping: Mix together all ingredients of topping and sprinkle over the top of cake mixture.

Bake at 350° for 35 minutes until top is brown and crusty. **Serves 12.**

Serve cake with cranberry juice or coffee.

FRUIT PIZZA

Paula M.
(Mrs. O. Luke, III) Davis
Dallas, TX

Our children love to make the designs for this delicious dessert. Their creativity really shines through! These pizzas make an especially festive dessert for the Fourth of July.

"It's as much fun as it is good!" Meredith (age 7½).

Crust:

½ cup butter or margarine
½ cup shortening
1½ cups sugar
2 eggs
2¾ cups flour
2 teaspoons cream of tartar
1 teaspoon baking soda
¼ teaspoon salt

Cream:

2 packages (8 ounces each) creamed cheese
1 cup sugar

Topping:

Assorted fresh fruit: strawberries, blueberries, bananas and grapes, cut into slices.

Mix together butter or margarine, shortening, sugar and eggs. Mix in remaining ingredients. Press into two round pizza pans sprayed with cooking spray. Bake at 350° for 15 minutes. Let cool. Mix together cream cheese and sugar and spread over crust. Cover with assorted fresh fruit. **Serves 10 to 12.**

Serve Fruit Pizza with dollop of whipped cream.

JULY 4TH FLAG CAKE

Sharon L. Whitley
Frisco, TX

My birthday is July 3rd, and each year we have a large family get-together on July 4th. My nieces and children have a great time decorating this cake, becoming more and more creative each year with the American flag.

2 packages (16 ounces each) pound cake mix
1½ cups milk
4 large eggs
3 cups cream, whipped
⅓ cup powdered sugar
1½ teaspoons vanilla extract
1½ pints blueberries
2½ pints raspberries

Preheat oven to 350°. Grease and flour a 13x9-inch baking pan. In large bowl, beat both boxes of pound cake mix with milk and eggs until blended. Pour into pan. Bake 45 to 50 minutes until toothpick inserted in center of cake comes out clean. Cool in pan on wire rack 15 minutes. Loosen edges; invert onto rack; cool completely.

When cake is cool, beat whipping cream, powdered sugar and vanilla extract until stiff peaks form, reserving a cup for piping. Place cake on large platter or tray; spread whipped cream mixture on sides and top of cake. Arrange blueberries and raspberries on top of cake to resemble the American flag, with blueberries representing the stars' background and leaving space between each "stripe" of raspberries. Spoon remaining mixture into decorating bag with medium-sized star tip; pipe 6 lines between raspberries to represent the white stripes on flag. Then pipe decorative border around bottom edge of cake. Refrigerate until ready to serve. **Serves 30.**

Serve cake with chilled lemonade.

HALLOWEEN DROPS

R. Jolly Brown
Arlington, VA

These are a wonderful treat for school Halloween parties—plus a wonderful source of vitamin A and fiber.

"Tastes like pumpkin pie, only better, cuz it's a cookie."

2½ tablespoons margarine
¼ cup granulated sugar
¼ cup brown sugar, packed
1 egg
¾ cup pumpkin, cooked and sieved
1 teaspoon vanilla extract
¾ cup whole wheat flour
1 teaspoon baking powder
¼ teaspoon baking soda
1 teaspoon cinnamon
¼ teaspoon nutmeg
¼ teaspoon ginger
½ cup raisins

In a mixing bowl, cream margarine with sugars. Beat in egg, pumpkin and vanilla. Sift together dry ingredients and spices in bowl. Stir in raisins. Drop by teaspoonfuls onto lightly greased baking sheets. Bake in 375° oven for 10 to 12 minutes. Cool. **Makes 2 dozen.**

Serve with vanilla bean ice cream.

GRANDMOTHER'S POPCORN BALLS

Susan Mullins Tipler
Birmingham, AL

My ten-year-old, Andrew, recommends this recipe—and his four-year-old brother Christopher agrees. I have made this on Halloween since before they were born—because my Grandmother Johnson always made them on Halloween.

Andrew says the popcorn balls are *"AWESOME! Everybody likes to trick-or-treat at our house!"*

P.S.: A SAD NOTE: This year we did not make popcorn balls because Andrew now has braces.

2 cups popcorn, unpopped
Salt to taste
2⅔ cups molasses
2 cups granulated sugar
1 teaspoon soda

Set out all ingredients before you begin. Pop the corn in batches, and salt lightly. In a large heavy saucepan, cook molasses and sugar until you can spin a thread, or until mixture reaches about 290° on a candy thermometer. Stir constantly. Add soda. It will foam up. Pour mixture over the popped corn and mix it quickly with a buttered spoon. When you are sure it is cool enough to touch, butter your hands and shape into balls while still very warm. When cool, wrap in squares of plastic wrap and tie with Halloween ribbons. **Makes 30.**

Serve popcorn balls with chilled soda.

PUMPKIN PIE CAKE

Suanne Karlinski
San Juan Capistrano, CA

This Halloween/Thanksgiving recipe comes from a dear friend of my mother's. As a child, I associated this delicious seasonal treat with any special fall activity, party or dinner. Now my children love it and enjoy making it with me.

1 can (16 ounces) pumpkin
1 can (12 ounces) evaporated milk
3 eggs
4 teaspoons pumpkin pie spice
½ teaspoon salt
1 cup sugar
1 yellow cake mix
2 cups pecans, chopped
1½ cups butter, melted

Mix together the pumpkin, milk, eggs, pumpkin pie spice, salt and sugar. Pour this mixture into a 9x13-inch pan. Sprinkle yellow cake mix over the top. Then sprinkle chopped pecans over cake mix. Pour melted butter over top. Bake in preheated 350° oven for 1 hour or until brown on top and inserted toothpick comes out clean. **Serves 12.**

Serve with a dollop of cinnamon whipped cream (stir 1 teaspoon cinnamon into 2 cups whipped cream).

HALLOWEEN CUPCAKES

Mrs. Robin Nigro
White Plains, NY

These Halloween cupcakes are a lot of fun to decorate and even better to eat. You can use almost anything to decorate them, but we like to use just plain old black licorice laces and Halloween candy corn.

Cupcakes:

1 cup granulated sugar
¼ cup vegetable oil
2 eggs
¾ cup canned pumpkin
1½ cups flour
1 teaspoon baking powder
½ teaspoon baking soda
¼ teaspoon ground cloves
¼ teaspoon cinnamon
¼ teaspoon nutmeg
½ teaspoon salt
½ cup walnuts, chopped

Icing:

4 ounces cream cheese
3 tablespoons butter, unsalted
1½ cups powdered sugar
½ teaspoon vanilla extract
1 teaspoon fresh lemon juice
2 to 3 drops orange food coloring

Cupcakes: Preheat oven to 400°. Generously grease a 12-muffin tin. Blend sugar, oil, eggs and pumpkin in a small bowl. Sift together dry ingredients in another bowl. Quickly stir together both mixtures and then fold in walnuts. Fill prepared muffin cups ⅔ full and bake for 18 to 20 minutes or until golden brown. To test for doneness, use a toothpick: when the toothpick comes out clean, muffins are done. Remove from oven and let muffins cool a few minutes in the pan before removing.

Icing: Cream the cream cheese and butter together in a mixing bowl. Add the powdered sugar and continue beating until smoothly blended. Stir in vanilla, lemon juice and food coloring. For a quick-fix method use any prepared vanilla icing and add 2 to 3 drops of orange food coloring. Decorate as you like with black licorice laces and candy corn. **Serves 12.**

Serve cupcakes with hot cinnamon tea.

PUMPKIN CREAM PIE

Mrs. Ronald C. Prati, Sr.
Dallas, TX

This recipe has been in our family for three generations. My mother, Mary LeNoir Giuffrida passed it on from her mother, Agnes McGrath LeNoir of Savannah, Georgia. The holidays would not be the same without it.

¾ cup sugar
2 tablespoons cornstarch
1 teaspoon cinnamon
½ teaspoon ground nutmeg
½ teaspoon ground ginger
¼ teaspoon ground cloves
½ teaspoon salt
2 cups evaporated milk
1 can (16 ounces) pumpkin
2 large eggs, separated
2 additional egg whites
¼ cup sugar
1 (9-inch) pie shell, baked

Mix sugar, cornstarch and spices in the top of a double boiler. Slowly stir in milk and pumpkin until well blended. Heat over boiling water for 20 minutes, stirring frequently. Remove from heat and slowly stir in slightly beaten egg yolks, a small amount at a time to keep from curdling. Return to heat and cook for 3 to 4 minutes, stirring constantly. Cool and pour into baked pie shell.

Beat egg whites until stiff and gradually add ¼ cup sugar to make meringue. Spread meringue on top of pumpkin mixture, being careful to seal edges to crust with a spatula. Bake at 450° for 3 to 5 minutes or until lightly browned. Let cool to room temperature before serving. Refrigerate after several hours. **Serves 8 to 10.**

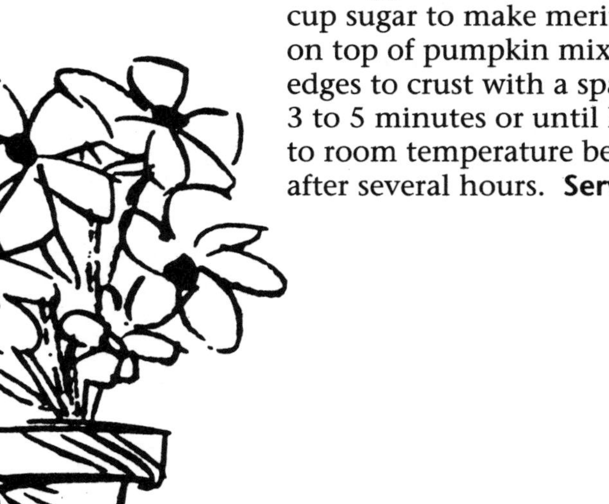

PUMPKIN RICE PUDDING

Jim Nedohon
Arlington, VA

This has been a family favorite for several generations. As soon as pumpkin season starts, the kids and adults look forward to this rich and easy dessert. The first batch of the season usually disappears during the first day. Even if the kids don't like pumpkin pie, they'll love this way of eating pumpkin.

3 cups fresh pumpkin, seeded, peeled and diced in ¼-inch cubes
1 cup water
6 cups milk
½ cup sugar
¼ teaspoon salt
1 cup white rice
2 teaspoons vanilla extract
¼ teaspoon ground nutmeg

Cook diced pumpkin with 1 cup of water in a covered medium sauce pan until just tender, about 10 minutes. Drain, let cool and set aside. In a heavy 3-quart saucepan combine milk, sugar, salt and rice over medium heat. Stir frequently and heat until mixture begins to simmer, then reduce to low heat. Cover and simmer for 1 hour, stirring occasionally until rice is tender. Remove from heat and combine vanilla, nutmeg and reserved pumpkin with rice mixture. Cover and chill very well before serving. **Serves 12.**

Lightly sprinkle with ground cinnamon before serving.

CRANBERRY CASSEROLE

Cynthia Keller
Dallas, TX

In my husband's family, this recipe has been given to every new bride since the early 1900s. It's a great way to get children to eat cranberries.

"It makes my tongue smile."

2 cups raw cranberries, chopped
3 apples, unpeeled and chopped
¼ cup water
1½ cups oatmeal
½ cup brown sugar
⅓ cup flour
⅓ cup pecans, chopped
⅓ cup margarine, melted

Mix cranberries, apples and water. Pour into a 2-quart buttered casserole. Mix together remaining ingredients and spoon onto cranberry mixture. Bake at 350° for 45 minutes. **Serves 6.**

Serve casserole with smoked turkey or with ice cream as a dessert.

HOLIDAY CRANBERRY MOLD

La Don G. Hix
Villa Park, CA

A festive Holiday Cranberry Mold that's been in our family for years. I surround it with holly and fresh cranberries, and it's always a hit.

2 cups fresh cranberries
2 cups sugar
1 package (6 ounces) strawberry gelatin
3½ cups boiling water
1 cup walnuts, chopped
1 can (20 ounces) pineapple, crushed and drained
Holly and berries

Grind cranberries; marinate in sugar for 2 hours. Mix gelatin with boiling water. Chill until syrupy. Stir in cranberry mixture, walnuts and pineapple. Pour into 6½-cup mold, chill until firm. Unmold onto a plate; surround with holly and berries. **Serves 6.**

Serve as side dish for Thanksgiving.

PHYLLO CRANBERRY CUP

Chef Renee Bajeux
Four Seasons Hotel
Beverly Hills, CA

3 sheets phyllo dough, thawed
2 tablespoons butter, melted
1 cup Ricotta cheese
2 teaspoons sugar
1 cup cranberry sauce

Unfold 3 sheets of phyllo dough and brush each layer with butter. Cut each sheet into 6 square pieces, place squares in mini-muffin pan and bake at 350° for 15 minutes or until lightly browned. Combine Ricotta cheese, sugar and cranberry sauce. Mix well. Fill each prepared phyllo cup with the cranberry mixture. Garnish with fresh cranberry and mint leaf. **Serves 6.**

THANKSGIVING CRANBERRY SALAD

Lynette H. King
Mineral Wells, TX

My mother (Mrs. Inex Roland Holman) serves this every Thanksgiving. It is a tradition which began over fifty years ago in our family. Our family reunions are each November during the holiday, and now all of the children, grandchildren and great-grandchildren have been told to dip a spoonful of salad onto their plates. Our best quote was from one child to another, *"You have to taste the cranberries, just like black-eyed peas on New Year's Day!"*

1 package (16 ounces) cranberries, ground
1¼ cups sugar
1 cup pineapple, crushed and drained
1 package (10½ ounces) marshmallows
1 cup pecan pieces
1 carton (8 ounces) whipping cream, whipped

Mix together all ingredients, folding in whipped cream last. **Serves 8.**

Great side dish for smoked turkey.

STRAWBERRY-CRANBERRY SALAD

Delores (Mrs. Thomas) Wehling
St. Charles, IL

It has become a tradition that I serve this family favorite with our Thanksgiving Day dinner.

Salad:

1 package (6 ounces) strawberry gelatin
2 cups boiling water
1 package (16 ounces) frozen strawberries
1 package (10 ounces) frozen cranberry or cranberry-orange relish, thawed
1 can (15¼ ounces) crushed pineapple, well-drained

Topping:

1 package (3 ounces) cream cheese
16 large marshmallows, quartered
1 cup whipping cream

Salad: In a 3-quart casserole dissolve, strawberry gelatin in boiling water. Add frozen strawberries, frozen cranberry or cranberry-orange relish and crushed pineapple. Refrigerate until set.

Topping: For topping, combine cream cheese, marshmallows and whipping cream and chill overnight. Before serving, beat topping with electric mixer until stiff. Spread mixture over gelatin. Cut into squares to serve. **Serves 8.**

This salad is delicious with any fowl.

TART AND SWEET CRANBERRY BREAD

Joyce Dickerson
Coral Gables, FL

I found this recipe in the newspaper in Virginia when my children were toddlers. They loved it then and beg for it now during the holidays. I make it as a holiday gift for friends and neighbors and have given out the recipe countless times.

"We eat this for dessert and sometimes for breakfast, too. What makes it is the buttery sauce."

Cranberry bread:

2 cups flour
1 cup sugar
2 teaspoons baking powder
½ teaspoon salt
⅔ cup evaporated milk
⅓ cup water
1 tablespoon butter or margarine, melted
2 cups fresh cranberries

Buttery sweet sauce:

½ cup butter or margarine
1 cup sugar
⅔ cup evaporated milk
1 teaspoon vanilla extract

Cranberry bread: Combine all dry ingredients in mixing bowl. Add milk, water, butter and stir well. Add cranberries and stir until well mixed. Spread into buttered 9x5-inch loaf pan. Bake at 350° for 1 hour. Cool 10 minutes; then remove from pan.

Buttery sweet sauce: In small saucepan, melt butter or margarine. Add sugar and milk. Heat to rolling boil. Boil for 1 minute, stirring constantly. Remove from heat and add vanilla. Serve warm over bread. Refrigerate leftover sauce. Bread can be refrigerated for several weeks or can be frozen. **Serves 8.**

Serve bread with warmed buttery sweet sauce and spiced tea.

BE BE'S PUMPKIN BREAD

Michèle d'Arlin Lynch
Los Angeles, CA

Pumpkin bread was a Thanksgiving tradition in my husband's family. It was the only thing in his refrigerator when we met and started dating. Now my daughter Nicole and I make it together on Thanksgiving. Nicole takes it to her preschool class; both kids and adults love it.

1 cup vegetable oil
3 cups sugar
2 cups canned pumpkin
⅔ cup water
3½ cups flour
2 teaspoons baking soda
1 teaspoon salt, optional
2 teaspoons cinnamon
1 whole nutmeg, finely grated
⅔ cup raisins

Preheat oven to 350°. Mix together oil, sugar, pumpkin and water. Sift dry ingredients together, and combine with pumpkin mixture. Beat with mixer until smooth and add raisins.

Rinse, dry and then grease and flour 3, one-pound coffee cans. Fill each can half-way full with batter. Bake at 350° for approximately 1 hour and 15 minutes or until browned on top. It is important to test for doneness with cake tester. **Serves 8 to 10.**

Slice bread and serve with flavored cream cheese.

SWEET 'N CRUNCHY PUMPKIN CASSEROLE

Mrs. S. C. (Sam) Schultz
Marietta, GA

I tried this instead of yams one time many years ago, and it was an instant hit.

1 can (16 ounces) pumpkin
1 cup miniature marshmallows
½ stick butter or margarine
3 eggs
1 teaspoon vanilla extract
⅔ cup granulated sugar
¼ cup milk
¼ teaspoon nutmeg

Topping:
½ stick butter
½ cup brown sugar
1 cup graham crackers, crumbled
1 cup pecans, chopped

Combine all ingredients except topping in a 2-quart saucepan; heat and stir until blended and hot. Remove and whip mixture. Pour into baking dish and cook in a 375° oven for 20 minutes.

Topping: Melt butter or margarine and sugar together. Combine with crumbled graham crackers and chopped pecans and spread on top of baked casserole. Return to oven for 5 more minutes to brown. **Serves 6 to 8.**

Serve with ham and steamed green beans with pearl onions.

PEANUT BUTTER ICE CREAM PIE

Constance A. Barnes
Merrillville, IN

This recipe was given to me in 1977 by my mother. It was usually served on Thanksgiving to children who didn't care for pumpkin pie.

My son Kris says, *"I like it even better than pizza."*

1½ cups graham cracker crumbs
⅓ cup butter, melted
¼ cup sugar
1 quart vanilla ice cream, softened
1 cup peanut butter
½ pint whipping cream, whipped
Graham cracker crumbs, roasted peanuts, chopped for garnish

Combine crumbs, butter and sugar. Press into 9-inch pie plate. Chill. Soften ice cream so it can be stirred with a spoon. Stir peanut butter into ice cream. Fold whipped cream into mixture until well blended. Pour into shell. If desired, sprinkle with more graham cracker crumbs and peanuts. Place in freezer to harden. If storing in freezer for more than a few hours, cover with freezer wrap. **Serves 8.**

APPLE PUDDING

Alene Nardick
Northbrook, IL

I got this recipe from my mother-in-law. It's good any time of the year, but it's great at Thanksgiving for the kids since they usually won't touch cranberry sauce.

2 cans (20 ounces each) apple pie filling
4 eggs, slightly beaten
1 tablespoon lemon juice
1 cup sugar
¾ cup vegetable oil
2 cups sugar-coated corn flakes

Blend together apple pie filling, eggs, lemon juice, sugar and oil. Arrange in a lightly greased 9x12-inch baking dish. Cover generously with sugared flakes. Bake at 350° for 1 hour. **Serves 8.**

Serve pudding with cinnamon ice cream.

DUTCH BABY PANCAKE

Sara M. (Mrs. Ted F.) Dunham
Marfa, TX

A favorite recipe for Christmas morning here at the Barrel Springs Ranch. I think everyone will enjoy this sweet pancake which is easy to make and delicious.

½ cup flour
½ cup milk
2 eggs, lightly beaten
Pinch of nutmeg
6 tablespoons butter or margarine
2 tablespoons powdered sugar
1 lemon, juiced

Preheat oven to 425°. Combine flour, milk, eggs and nutmeg. Beat lightly by hand, leaving the batter a little lumpy. Melt butter in a 12-inch heatproof baking dish or skillet. When hot, remove from oven and pour in batter. Bake 15 to 20 minutes, or until golden brown. Sprinkle with sugar and return to oven briefly. Drizzle lemon juice over sugar and serve immediately. Cut into wedges to serve. **Serves 2.**

Note: Recipe doubles easily.

FESTIVE APPLE SWEET POTATOES

Joyce Shlesinger
Atlanta, GA

My family and friends always look forward to our Thanksgiving and other holidays with silver platters of festive apple sweet potatoes.

10 large Granny Smith apples, washed, cored and cut in half
1 can (17 ounces) sweet potatoes
¼ cup dark corn syrup
1 teaspoon salt
¼ teaspoon cinnamon
16 miniature marshmallows
1 tablespoon lemon juice
¼ cup butter

Prepare apple shell halves by scooping out the apple until wall of apple is about half an inch thick, discard pulp. Mash sweet potatoes and combine with remaining ingredients, except melted butter. Blend thoroughly, then stuff apples to overflowing. Place in an ovenproof dish. Baste with melted butter. Place stuffed apples in a 350° oven. Bake 30 minutes or until soft but not mushy. **Serves 8 to 10.**

AUTUMN SQUASH

Mary Martens
Chesterfield, MO

Squash has been our traditional vegetable served at both Thanksgiving and Christmas for three generations.

1 (2 to 3 pounds) butternut squash
¼ cup butter or margarine
¼ teaspoon salt
1 tablespoon brown sugar
Pinch of white pepper
6 medium Jonathan apples, cored and sliced
1½ tablespoons shortening
¼ cup sugar
3 individual packages (1 1/16 ounces each) corn flakes, coarsely crushed
½ cup pecans, chopped
2 tablespoons butter, melted
½ cup brown sugar

Halve the squash, scrape out seeds. Steam for 30 minutes, or bake upside down on a piece of foil at 300° until tender. Scrape out pulp and mash or beat with a mixer until smooth. Add margarine, salt, brown sugar and white pepper.

Heat shortening in a skillet. Add the apples, sprinkle with sugar, cover and simmer on low heat until the apples are barely tender. Spread these in an 8-inch square or 9-inch round shallow casserole. Cover with squash mixture.

To prepare the topping, combine corn flakes, pecans, butter and sugar. Spoon on top of squash. Bake at 350° for about 12 to 15 minutes or until lightly browned. Serve piping hot.
Serves 8.

Serve as a side dish with smoked turkey or ham.

CORN PUDDIN'

Richard Ford Thompson
Dallas, TX

This wonderful pudding is a great way to serve corn. It is an easy addition to any holiday or family gathering. I give you this recipe with love and happiness.

1 can (17 ounces) whole kernel corn, drained
1 can (17 ounces) creamed corn
1 teaspoon sugar
½ teaspoon salt
¼ teaspoon cracked fresh pepper
2 tablespoons butter or margarine, melted

Stir all ingredients together and pour into a 2-quart casserole dish which has been sprayed with nonstick cooking spray. Bake 45 minutes at 375° uncovered. **Serves 6.**

Serve pudding as a side dish to roast beef or chicken.

CREAMY CORN

Sheri Best
Newport Beach, CA

I've made this corn for the Thanksgiving and Christmas holidays for about ten years. It's always been a huge hit, especially with my four children.

1 package (10 ounces) frozen corn
1 cup half-and-half
1 teaspoon salt
2 teaspoons butter
2 teaspoons flour
¼ cup Parmesan cheese, grated
2 tablespoons butter for top

Thaw frozen corn in colander for 1 hour. Preheat oven to 350°. Put corn in saucepan with half-and-half. Bring to a boil, then turn heat to low and cook slowly for 5 minutes. Remove from heat and add salt. In a separate pan, melt 2 teaspoons butter and stir in flour. Don't let it turn brown. Stir butter-flour mixture into corn and cook over low heat until slightly thickened. Pour into baking dish. Sprinkle with cheese and dot with butter. Bake at 350° for 10 minutes. Recipe may be easily multiplied. **Serves 6 to 8.**

The corn is great with ham, chicken or beef.

BROCCOLI CASSEROLE

Ruth Wander
Highland Park, IL

"Do I have to wait for Thanksgiving to have the broccoli casserole?"

1 pound VELVEETA® cheese, melted
1 stick margarine, melted
5 packages (16 ounces each) frozen chopped broccoli, cooked and drained
1 teaspoon salt
1 teaspoon pepper

Topping:

1 stack RITZ® crackers, crumbled
1 stick margarine, melted

Melt the cheese with the margarine. Mix all ingredients except topping. Place into a 3-quart casserole. Place crackers over top of broccoli mixture. Melt margarine and drizzle over the top. Bake in 350° oven for 25 to 30 minutes. **Serves 12.**

Serve as a side dish with honey-baked ham or add two cups of cooked, cubed chicken and serve as an entrée.

EGGPLANT CHEESE PUFF

Vicki Rosholt
Minneapolis, MN

This puffs up beautifully and looks delicious on the buffet table.

2 cups eggplant, diced
1 cup garbanzo beans, drained
⅓ cup onion, chopped
1 pound turkey sausage
1 tablespoon chili powder
¼ teaspoon salt
¼ teaspoon pepper
1 tablespoon butter or margarine
½ cup flour
½ cup milk
2 eggs, lightly beaten
¼ cup Cheddar cheese, shredded
1 medium tomato, unpeeled and cut into 12 wedges

Coat a large nonstick skillet with cooking spray; place over medium heat until hot. Add eggplant, beans, turkey sausage and onion; sauté until onion is tender and sausage is cooked, stirring frequently. Stir in the spices, remove from heat and set aside.

Coat a 9-inch pie plate with cooking spray; add margarine. Bake at 475° until margarine melts. Combine flour, milk and eggs in medium bowl and stir well, using a wire whisk. Pour mixture into pie plate, do not stir.

Bake at 475° for 12 minutes or until puffed and golden. Spoon eggplant mixture into puffed pancake and bake for an additional 2 minutes. Remove from oven and sprinkle with cheese. Top with tomato wedges. **Serves 4.**

Serve with spinach salad and crusty bread.

THANKSGIVING SWEET POTATOES

Gwen Dixie
Dallas, TX

I worked out this recipe through trial and error. I'm big on making things look good. I'll go to a lot of trouble since I believe we eat with the eye first. I have four children, ages thirty-two, thirty, twenty-one and seventeen. They more or less take cooking for granted, but they are big vegetable eaters.

My nieces always say, *"Heavy on the sweet potatoes."*

6 sweet potatoes or 2 cans (29 ounces each) sweet potatoes
¾ stick butter or margarine
½ cup of evaporated milk or cream
½ tablespoon nutmeg
1 tablespoon cinnamon
1 tablespoon cardamom
1 cup brown sugar
½ cup orange juice
1 dozen oranges or tangerines
12 large marshmallows, halved

Wash and boil the potatoes until tender. Peel and mash. Beat in the butter or margarine until melted. Add milk or cream to mixture. Add spices and sugar and beat. Add orange juice to the mixture. Cut the oranges or tangerines in half and take out most of the fruit with a sharp knife (this can be saved for the fruit salad). Don't worry about getting all of the fruit out of the oranges as it will add to the taste. Put the potato mixture into the empty shells. Add a marshmallow on top.

Hint: If you cut the marshmallows in half, use a pair of scissors dipped in powdered sugar to keep them from sticking.

Refrigerate until ready to serve. Place them into a 350° oven for 5 to 8 minutes or until the marshmallow is browned and the potatoes are heated through. **Makes 24.**

For an edible garnish, serve these shells around the turkey.

SWEET POTATO BALLS

Mickie Rabinowitz
Plantation, FL

This recipe was extracted from a chef of a hotel in Puerto Rico (under duress).

Our son was disappointed when he realized that *"the balls don't bounce!"*

2 pounds sweet potatoes
1½ quarts boiling water
1 teaspoon salt
½ cup coconut milk
3 cups sugar
2 egg yolks

Wash and quarter sweet potatoes. Cook in water with salt for 40 minutes. Drain, peel, and mash immediately.

Add coconut milk, sugar and egg yolks, stirring rapidly. Cook to a boil, stirring constantly with a wooden spoon in a back-and-forth motion. Lower heat to medium and continue cooking for about ½ hour or until the mixture separates completely from the pan. Shape into small balls. Sprinkle lightly with cinnamon. **Makes 36.**

Serve with smoked turkey and cranberry sauce.

HOLIDAY RICE DRESSING

Becky Cervenka
Freeport, TX

This is one of the most popular dressings I have ever prepared. Every year I take this dressing to our family dinners at Thanksgiving and Christmas—by request.

1 pound sausage, ground
½ cup onion, diced
1 cup celery, cubed
1 cup rice, raw
2 packages LIPTON® chicken soup mix, or LIPTON® beefy onion soup mix
4½ cups water

Brown sausage in Dutch oven. Add onions and celery and cook slowly. Add rice and sauté until lightly browned. Prepare soup in a separate pot with 4½ cups water. Pour the soup over the sausage and rice mixture. Do NOT stir. Put a tight lid on pot. Bake at 350° for one hour. **Serves 6 to 8.**

This dressing is also delicious made with ground beef and beef soup mix.

CHALLAH

Mrs. Leonard Rosenberg
Houston, TX

My recipe for Challah was taught to me forty years ago by my aunt. I bake Challah for holidays and the Sabbath. I also made Challah for five hundred people for each of my two daughters' weddings. My grandchildren love to help me bake and enjoy eating it. I have baked this bread with each of my five children and six grandchildren in their early school years. And now I would like to share it with others.

"Grandma can we bake Challah?" And, "Do you have any in the freezer now?"

3 packages yeast
2 cups warm water
10 cups flour
½ cup sugar
1 cup oil
2 teaspoons salt
1 egg, beaten
1 tablespoon poppy seeds

Dissolve yeast in warm water. In a separate bowl combine flour, sugar, oil and salt. When yeast is dissolved, pour into flour mixture. Mix well. Brush the inside of a separate bowl with oil and roll the dough until coated. Cover with a tea towel and let rise in a warm place for 1 hour. Turn onto a floured board. Knead until smooth, adding flour until the dough is not sticky. Shape into 3 loaves—you can use any shape pans or a cookie sheet. Grease pans. Brush the bread with a beaten egg and sprinkle with poppy seed. Let the bread rise for 1 hour in a warm place. Bake at 325° until golden brown. Bread freezes well. **Makes 3 loaves.**

Great as a holiday gift or with any meal.

HAMAN'S HATS (HAMANTASCHEN)

Mrs. Adinah W. Raskas
St. Louis, MO

Haman's Hats are the most popular sweets made from flour and served on the Jewish holiday called Purim. One legend tells us that the three corners of the cookie represent Abraham, Isaac, and Jacob, the founding fathers of Judaism. Although Hamantaschen are usually filled with poppy-seed or prune filling, these are filled with a strawberry filling or even chocolate chips.

Dough:

½ cup shortening
¼ cup oil
¾ cup sugar
¼ cup orange juice
1 teaspoon vanilla extract
2 eggs
2 teaspoons baking powder
Pinch of salt
2½ cups flour

Filling:

½ cup strawberry preserves
⅛ to ¼ cup white raisins
⅛ to ¼ cup walnuts, chopped
2 teaspoons lemon juice

Cream shortening, oil, sugar and orange juice. Add remaining ingredients. Mix well. Form dough into a ball and divide the dough into two cylinders, 3 inches in diameter. Chill dough.

Cut ⅛-inch slices of dough and roll them out. Place 1 teaspoon of filling in the center of each round. Draw the edges up at three points to form a triangle. Place the triangles on a greased baking sheet. Bake at 375° for 12 to 16 minutes or until golden brown. **Makes 3 dozen.**

Note: You can use 1 teaspoon of chocolate chips per cookie as an alternative filling.

KASHA AND BOWS

Eileen H. Swartz
Swampscott, MA

This side dish was and is still served in our home on almost every Jewish holiday.

My daughter always says, *"It can't be a holiday unless we have Kasha and Bows."*

1 cup water
1 cup chicken broth
1 egg
1 cup kasha, roasted buckwheat, medium granulation
1 stick butter or margarine
1 medium onion, finely diced
2 cups egg noodle bows, cooked
Salt and pepper to taste

Heat water and broth to boiling. In a separate bowl, beat egg lightly, add kasha and mix well. Melt butter or margarine in large pan and lightly brown onions. Add kasha and brown. Add boiling liquid mixture, cover pot tightly and simmer 8 to 11 minutes or until kasha is tender and all liquid is absorbed. Add cooked egg noodle bows and salt and pepper to taste. **Serves 4.**

Serve Kasha and Bows with a crisp green salad.

CHOCOLATE-COVERED MATZOS

Beverly Kabakoff Adilman
Chicago, IL

Due to the dietary laws of Passover, we are limited as to what kind of treats we can have. So we decided to create our own. Since everyone likes chocolate, it was only logical to take the traditional Passover food, matzo, and cover it with chocolate. My husband Ron, our daughter Joree and I have started our own family tradition.

My daughter Joree says, *"When Passover time rolls around, all the kids can't wait for me to bring my Chocolate-Covered Matzos to school."*

1 pound milk chocolate

9 whole pieces of regular matzos

Break chocolate into small pieces and place in double boiler and slowly bring temperature up to 110° to 120°. When temperature is attained, remove from burner and slowly stir for 1 minute while bringing temperature back down to 90° to 100°. Using a frosting spatula, generously spread the chocolate over one side of the matzo, making sure the area is covered. Place on waxed paper for 30 minutes. If you desire, melted white chocolate can be used to decorate or personalize each piece by drizzling the white onto the dark, making different holiday designs. Refrigerate for 2 hours. For the real chocolate lovers, both sides of the matzo can be covered. **Makes 9.**

Serve matzos with hot mint tea.

CHOPPED CHICKEN LIVERS

Evy Rappaport
Beverly Hills, CA

My son began testing this chopped chicken liver recipe when in his high chair. He much preferred it to baby food. Today, sixteen years later, he is still my most severe liver critic!

"This time, it is truly the best you have ever, ever made."

2 tablespoons butter
2 tablespoons olive oil
5 pounds chicken livers, sautéed
Seasoned salt, pepper, thyme, and garlic to taste
1 large onion, chopped
¼ cup Grand Marnier
18 eggs, hard-boiled and chopped

In sauté pan heat butter and olive oil. Season livers with above spices and sauté with onion for 20 minutes. Add ¼ cup Grand Marnier. Sauté another 5 minutes and remove from pan. Blend sautéed livers, onion and pan juices in food processor with sharp blade. In large bowl combine eggs and liver. **Serves 20 to 25.**

Note: Alcohol content evaporates when cooked. Use of alcohol subject to own discretion and dietary restrictions.

Serve as a first course with cocktail rye bread.

CHOCOLATE MINT BROWNIES

Governor Ann W. Richards
Austin, TX

My passion for chocolate has become legendary, and I can assure you that these brownies will not disappoint. The layer of peppermint icing provides a nice variation from your run-of-the-mill chocolate brownie and makes them perfect for holiday parties or as a light dessert. And speaking from personal experience, they're a big hit with grandkids!

Brownies:

½ cup margarine, melted
2 squares unsweetened chocolate, melted
2 eggs
½ teaspoon salt
1 cup sugar
½ cup flour
1 teaspoon vanilla extract
½ cup nuts, chopped

Filling:

4 tablespoons butter
1 cup powdered sugar
1 teaspoon peppermint extract
1 drop green food coloring

Icing:

1 tablespoon butter
1 square unsweetened chocolate

Combine melted butter and chocolate; let cool. Beat together eggs, salt and sugar. Add chocolate mixture. Add remaining ingredients. Pour into a greased 9x13-inch baking dish. Bake at 325° for 20 to 25 minutes. Cool.

Mix together all filling ingredients and spread on top of cooled brownies. Refrigerate until cold.

Melt chocolate with butter and spread over cold brownies. Refrigerate and cut into squares. **Serves 8.**

Serve brownies with peppermint ice cream.

CHRISTMAS EVE LOG

Carol Baker
San Bernadino, CA

I have been making this every Christmas Eve since 1965. On Christmas Eve, we have to have our Yule log with our eggnog. This has been a tradition in our family for over thirty years.

Cake:

1 cup cake flour
¼ cup cocoa
1 teaspoon baking powder
¼ teaspoon salt
3 eggs
1 cup sugar
⅓ cup water
1 teaspoon vanilla extract

Filling:

2 cups powdered sugar
2 eggs
¼ cup milk
4 squares unsweetened chocolate, melted
2 tablespoons soft butter

Bark:

2 squares unsweetened chocolate, shaved

Cake: Grease 10x15x1-inch jelly roll pan; line with greased waxed paper. Heat oven to 350°. Sift flour, cocoa, baking powder and salt together. Set aside. Beat eggs until stiff and lemon-colored. Gradually add sugar, beating until mixture is very thick. Stir in water and vanilla, then fold in flour mixture. Spread batter in pan. Bake 10 to 15 minutes or until center springs back when pressed with finger. Remove paper; trim edges of cake. Cover the cake with a dish towel. Roll up at once, rolling the towel with the cake.

Filling: Combine the powdered sugar, eggs, milk, unsweetened chocolate and soft butter. Beat at high speed until well blended. Place bowl in pan of ice water and continue beating for 3 minutes or until spreading consistency. Unroll cake. Spread with two-thirds of the filling and re-roll placing seam side down. Spread the remaining filling over top and sides of roll.

Bark: Place unsweetened chocolate on a square of foil in a warm oven. When soft, spread in a thin layer and chill. Lift chocolate off foil and crumble into small pieces, chill again and quickly sprinkle on top and sides of roll, covering cake with chocolate "bark," then dust the top with powdered sugar. **Serves 8 to 10.**

Serve log with cold milk or eggnog.

GRANDMA'S PEANUT BRITTLE

Dr. Smith Gaddy
Rolla, MO

This is an old family recipe passed down for generations and is an annual holiday tradition. Throughout the years, all of the kids have complained bitterly about working with the hot messy candy. Daughter Erin (now married) says that now she realizes why we did this. It brings the family closer and she is going to continue the tradition in her family.

2 cups sugar
1 cup KARO® corn syrup
2 cups unroasted peanuts
1 tablespoon butter
1 teaspoon baking soda

Heat sugar and syrup until a light caramel color, or until 320° to 350° is reached on candy thermometer. Add unroasted peanuts, butter and soda. Mix thoroughly and pour on greased cookie sheet. Spread thinly and allow to harden. When hard, break into pieces. **Serves 8.**

Serve as a dessert by crumbling brittle over ice cream.

FUDGE COOKIES

Margaret H. McFarland
Houston, TX

My mother always made these at Christmastime and kept a jar full. Once I asked my college-age son what he needed to have it be a successful Christmas for him. He replied, *"A tree and fudge cookies."*

2 tablespoons margarine
3 cups chocolate chips
1 can (14 ounces) sweetened condensed milk
1 cup flour, sifted
1 cup pecans, chopped
1 teaspoon vanilla extract

Preheat oven to 325°. Melt margarine and chocolate over boiling water. When melted, remove from heat and stir in sweetened condensed milk. Then add the flour and mix well. Add the nuts and vanilla. Drop by spoonfuls onto a greased baking sheet 2 inches apart. Bake for 15 minutes, being careful that cookies are still a little moist. **Makes 3 dozen.**

Serve cookies with cold milk or hot coffee.

18TH CENTURY GINGERBREAD COOKIES

Christine Elise Parrott
St. Louis, MO

This recipe is over two hundred years old. I have been making these every Christmas for twenty-three years. I tell all the neighborhood children it's baking day and to come by our house Christmas Eve day and pick from the gingerbread men on the tree.

"Are our Gingermen ready yet?"

2 cups flour, sifted
¼ teaspoon salt
½ teaspoon baking soda
1 teaspoon baking powder
1 teaspoon ginger
1 teaspoon cloves, ground
1½ teaspoons cinnamon
½ teaspoon nutmeg
½ cup liquid shortening
½ cup granulated sugar
½ cup molasses
1 egg yolk

Icing:

2 cups powdered sugar
½ teaspoon cream of tartar
3 egg whites
1 teaspoon vanilla extract
Food coloring

Sift all dry ingredients together, except sugar, and set aside. In a large bowl, mix liquid shortening, sugar and molasses until creamy and beat in egg yolk thoroughly. Add dry ingredients slowly. Roll dough into a ball. Dust waxed paper with flour and sprinkle top of dough ball with flour. Roll out to quarter inch thick. Cut out 5-inch to 6-inch gingerbread men. Grease cookie sheet. Preheat oven to 350° and bake 8 minutes. When cookies are cool, prepare icing.

Icing: Sift together powdered sugar and cream of tartar. Beat egg whites until stiff, then add vanilla. Add dry ingredients slowly. Add a drop of food coloring. Decorate men by outlining them with icing: make eyes, nose, mouth and buttons with icing. You can press raisins or silver candies into icing to highlight buttons, eyes and nose, if desired. Let icing set; then hang on tree or garland. **Makes 1 dozen.**

Note: If using for holiday decorating and hanging on the tree, cut hole in top of each cookie with a straw while still warm from baking.

SUGARPLUM CAKE

Jimmy & Patti Connors
Santa Ynez, CA

A close friend's recipe that we make at Christmastime.

1 cup vegetable oil
3 eggs
½ cup buttermilk
¾ cup prunes, stewed
1 teaspoon vanilla
1½ cups sugar
2½ cups flour
1 teaspoon salt
1 teaspoon baking soda
1 teaspoon allspice
1 teaspoon cinnamon
1 teaspoon nutmeg
1 cup pecans, chopped

Glaze:
1¼ cups sugar
1 stick butter
⅔ cup buttermilk
½ teaspoon baking soda

Cake: In a large mixing bowl, combine oil, eggs, buttermilk, prunes and vanilla. Mix well. Add sugar, flour, salt, baking soda, allspice, cinnamon and nutmeg. Mix to combine. Fold in nuts. Bake in a springform angel food pan which has been greased and floured. Bake at 300° for 1 hour.

Glaze: Near the end of the baking time, prepare glaze, timing this so that it is finished as soon as the cake comes out of the oven. In a large saucepan, combine sugar, butter, buttermilk and soda. Bring ingredients to a boil and cook 3 minutes. (Use large saucepan because glaze foams up when cooking.) Remove cake from oven and pour glaze over hot cake. Do not remove from pan until cake is cool. **Serves 12.**

Serve with hot cinnamon tea.

FABULOUS FUDGE

James D. Felter
Scottsdale, AZ

This recipe was found in an old recipe box that had been handed down to me from my great aunt Besse Gunkel. It has been a Christmas delight for years.

"Is this what makes the Felter family so very famous?. . . REALLY?"

2 cups marshmallow cream
3 cups sugar
1 can (12 ounces) evaporated milk
¾ cup butter
½ teaspoon salt
3 cups semisweet chocolate chips
1 cup English walnuts, chopped
2 teaspoons vanilla extract
Walnut halves for garnish

Place marshmallow cream, sugar, evaporated milk, butter and salt in a copper sauce pan. Bring to a slow boil over medium heat, stirring constantly. Boil 5 minutes, remove from heat. Stir in the chocolate chips, walnuts and vanilla. Pour ingredients into a buttered glass baking dish. Chill 3 hours, cut into squares, placing walnut half on top of each, then chill for an additional 24 hours. **Serves 36.**

Note: Must boil the full 5 minutes so fudge will harden properly.

Serve fudge with coffee, hot tea or cider.

Note: For adults, nuts may be marinated in cognac overnight before preparation. Pecans may be substituted.

SNOW PUDDING

Mrs. Anne E. Sullivan
Newburyport, MA

This recipe was given to me by my mother and was used frequently in the early '20s. I remember having this dessert at my grandmother's every Thanksgiving and Christmas and thinking that it was so much like real snow: white and fluffy and so good to eat. My daughter now uses the treat for the holidays and special dinners. All the children really adore the idea of eating a snow-like pudding!

Snow Pudding:

1 package granulated gelatin
¼ cup cold water
⅛ teaspoon salt
1 cup boiling water
1 cup sugar
¼ cup fresh lemon juice
3 egg whites, reserve yolks

Custard Sauce:

3 egg yolks
2 tablespoons sugar
Pinch of salt
1½ cups hot milk
½ teaspoon vanilla extract

Snow Pudding: Soak gelatin in cold water and add salt. Pour boiling water over it and stir until dissolved. Add sugar and lemon juice, and strain into a large bowl to cool. Refrigerate. Beat the egg whites until stiff. When the gelatin mixture has partially thickened in the refrigerator, remove and add the egg whites and whip until stiff enough to hold its shape. Refrigerate until firm and very cold.

Custard Sauce: In a double boiler, beat egg yolks slightly, add sugar, salt and milk. Cook on medium heat stirring constantly until thickened. Cool and add vanilla. **Serves 4.**

The children prefer this dessert plain; adults adore the custard sauce on it.

CHRISTMAS EVE CHOCOLATE PUNCH

Nancy (Mrs. Kent) Snyder
Laguna Beach, CA

When our children were small, they were so excited about the arrival of Santa on Christmas Eve, that an afternoon and early evening party seemed a good way to spend that time. This tradition has continued for twenty-two years. Chocolate Punch is the hit of the party—but be sure to use decaffeinated coffee or the children will never go to sleep and Santa can't come at a reasonable hour!

1½ cups instant decaffeinated coffee, powder or granules
1 cup instant hot chocolate mix
1 cup sugar
3 quarts hot water
1½ gallons vanilla ice cream, softened slightly
1 gallon chocolate ice cream, softened slightly
1 pint cream, whipped

Mix and dissolve together coffee, instant hot chocolate mix and sugar in hot water. Refrigerate in large container for 24 hours. When you're ready to serve, put chocolate liquid in punch bowl, add ice cream scoops and top with whipped cream. **Serves 48.**

Serve punch with iced holiday cookies.

THE CHILI THAT SAVED CHRISTMAS

Brady White
Los Angeles, CA

Mrs. C. would make this chili on Christmas Eve as Santa and his helpers prepared the sleigh and finished wrapping presents. One Christmas Eve in particular, Santa had a terrible cold and feared he wouldn't have the energy for the long night ahead. After a bowl of this delicious chili, Santa regained his strength and set out on his rounds. Ever since, this chili has been a tradition at Santa's house on every Christmas Eve. Personally, I think this is the best chili served this side of the North Pole.

Mrs. C, wife of "Santa to the Stars" says,
"So that's how Santa gets back up the chimney!"

4 tablespoons olive oil
½ cup medium onions, chopped
½ cup green peppers, diced
1 clove garlic, finely chopped
1 pound lean ground beef or turkey
1 can (6 ounces) tomato paste
2 teaspoons salt
2 cups tomatoes, canned
2 teaspoons salt
2 tablespoons chili powder
½ cup water
1 can (15½ ounces) dark red kidney beans, drained

Heat oil, add onions, green peppers and garlic. Sauté until golden brown. Add ground beef or turkey and stir until lightly browned. Add tomatoes, salt, chili powder and water. Cover saucepan and bring to a quick boil. Lower heat and simmer slowly for 30 minutes. Then add kidney beans and simmer 15 more minutes. **Serves 4 to 6 . . . or 8 tiny reindeer.**

Serve with corn bread or oyster crackers.

SO-HIGH TEA

Chuck & Marian Jones
Santa Barbara, CA

Writing in her journal, my daughter asked each one of my three grandsons, independently, what event around Christmastime had they enjoyed the most. All three answered *"Grandma's High Tea!"*

Proof positive that our illustrator's wife is equally creative in her own way. Here's her recipe/menu for the high tea that delighted their grandsons.

Platter of Assorted Sandwiches:

Deviled Egg Sandwiches:
6 eggs, hard-boiled and chopped
6 tablespoons mayonnaise
Salt and pepper, to taste
Dash of seasoning salt

Olive and Cream Cheese Sandwiches:
1 can (4¼ ounces) chopped black olives
1 package (3 ounces) cream cheese

Ham Sandwiches:
12 slices deli ham, thinly sliced (2 slices per sandwich)

Cucumber Sandwiches:
1 small cucumber, peeled and seeded, very thinly sliced

Large pot of tea (fresh-brewed or with tea bags) served with milk and sugar cubes
Bowl of PEPPERIDGE FARM® goldfish tiny crackers and butterfly tiny crackers
Plate of small bakery cookies appropriate to the occasion, or store-bought cookies such as OREOS®

To assemble sandwiches, take 2 large loaves of white bread, thinly sliced. Remove crust and spread each slice lightly with butter. Spread 6 slices with the egg mixture and top each with bread slice. Cut each diagonally into four sandwiches. Do the same for the other fillings. Cut the egg and olive in a diamond shape, and the ham and cucumber in a rectangle shape.
Serves 4 adults and **3 children.**

Serve with chinaware, tablecloth, lighted candles and flowers. Mix with conversation and joy.

CHAPTER EIGHT

ROLL OVER AND PLAY SICK

Some days the sniffles, coughs or the blahs just catch up with you, and a day away from school or office seems the best way to go. So, we hibernate, watch soaps, stack up the books and videos and wait for something comforting to come out of the kitchen on a tray. It could be anything from Milk Toast to bone-healing chicken soup or fruit slushes. We've got a lot of good-for-what-ails-you suggestions on these next pages.

MILK TOAST

Mrs. K. R. Tharp
Dallas, TX

Children in my family always looked forward to Milk Toast when *"under the weather."*

2 slices bread
2 teaspoons butter
1 cup milk

Toast and butter 2 slices of bread. In a pan, warm milk until just before boiling point. Pour over toast in soup bowl. Serve hot. **Serves 2.**

Serve toast with hot tea.

TOAST SHEEP

Marianne Waid
Atlanta, GA

From my mother from her mother in Germany.

2 slices white bread, toasted
3 teaspoons butter
2 tablespoons sugar
½ teaspoon cinnamon
¼ cup raisins, chopped
1 bunch grapes

Toast two slices of white bread and butter generously. Sprinkle with sugar and cinnamon. Cut into bite-sized pieces. Cut up a few raisins and make eyes for each "sheep." Arrange on a dish with a bunch of grapes in the center. **Serves 2.**

Serve with a tall glass of milk.

PAIN PERDU (LOST BREAD)

Mrs. William J. Nesbitt
Shreveport, LA

Pain Perdu is an old French means of using stale French bread. My aunt's cook always had it on my breakfast tray.

2 teaspoons cornstarch
1 cup milk
1 egg, beaten
3 tablespoons sugar
1 tablespoon butter
½ teaspoon nutmeg
½ teaspoon cinnamon
4 slices of stale French bread

Mix the cornstarch with 1 tablespoon of milk, set aside. In a bowl deep enough for the bread to be covered, combine the remaining milk, egg, sugar and spices, and add the cornstarch mixture. Soak the bread in the mixture until it is softened, then fry in butter until lightly browned on both sides. **Serves 2.**

Serve Pain Perdu sprinkled with powdered sugar.

MOTHER'S CHICKEN SOUP

Elizabeth Francis
Corwin Springs, MT

My parents taught me to cook German and Swiss dishes. This is a hearty soup for winter months of colds and flu or for Sunday night supper.

Broth:
- **2 quarts of water**
- **3 stalks celery, including leaves**
- **¼ bunch of parsley**
- **1 small onion, whole**
- **1 pound of chicken**

Soup:
- **1 cup celery, diced (to ½ inches)**
- **1 cup carrots, chopped (to 1½ inches)**
- **1 cup potatoes with skins, chopped**
- **¼ cup celery leaves, chopped**
- **2 cups rice, cooked**
- **½ cup parsley, chopped**
- **Salt and pepper to taste**

Broth: To prepare the broth, bring 2 quarts of water to a boil. Wash vegetables and chicken. Tie celery stalks and parsley with kitchen twine and add to boiling water with chicken and onion. Simmer for 1 hour. When the chicken is tender, strain the vegetables and chicken. Reserve both the chicken and the broth. Cool the broth in the refrigerator for 12 hours to congeal the fat.

Soup: Once the broth has chilled, remove the top layer of fat with a spoon. Prepare the vegetables for the soup. Bone and skin the chicken and cut it into 1-inch pieces. Bring the broth to a boil. Add the celery, celery leaves and carrots; lower heat and simmer broth for 5 minutes; add the potatoes and cook another 5 minutes. Add the chicken and rice. Cook together for 10 minutes. Season to taste. Just before serving, stir in chopped parsley. **Serves 8.**

Serve soup with cheese toast or oyster crackers.

STEAMED SEAFOOD EGG CUSTARD

Jing-Ru Chen
San Francisco, CA

Mom's secret recipe for colds.

3 eggs, beaten
¼ pound crabmeat, chopped
2 clams, chopped
¼ pound scallops, chopped
¼ pound shrimp, chopped
1 teaspoon salt
¾ cup water
1 tablespoon green onion, chopped
2 shitake mushrooms, cut into thin strips

Slightly beat eggs. Wash and chop seafood. Then mix with the beaten eggs, salt, water and chopped green onion. Put the mixture into a bowl, place in a bamboo steamer and steam at medium heat until eggs become translucent and tender. **Serves 2.**

Note: A vegetable steamer can be used.

Serve Egg Custard with steamed white rice.

CHICKEN STEW

Denise McCoy
Houston, TX

Great-great-uncle Tag would go hunting and bring home rabbits for supper. Great-great-aunt Bernice became tired of fried rabbit, so she created a family recipe for rabbit stew. It has been passed down from generation to generation until my grandmother substituted chicken for rabbit. The stew with chicken was even better!

6 large chicken breasts
1 can (14½ ounces) chicken broth
2 large onions, chopped
3 cans (16 ounces each) whole tomatoes, blended
1 can (17 ounces) kernel corn
1 can (17 ounces) creamed corn
Salt and pepper to taste

Place chicken in a Dutch oven; cover with water and bring to a boil. Remove chicken after it has cooked, reserving broth; let cool. Skin and bone chicken, chop meat and set aside. Add chicken broth, chopped onion and undrained corns to reserved broth. In a blender, chop tomatoes until fine and add to chicken broth mixture. Bring to a boil, stirring constantly. Reduce heat and simmer for 15 minutes. Add chicken and seasonings. Simmer another 15 minutes. Can be frozen. **Serves 8 to 10.**

Serve stew with jalapeño corn bread or wheat crackers.

EASY CHICKEN AND RICE CASSEROLE

Nancy Wright
Marietta, GA

My kids and all their friends ask for this.

1½ cups white rice, uncooked
1 can cream of mushroom soup
1 can cream of celery soup
1 can cream of chicken soup
1½ cans of water
6 to 8 chicken breasts, or assorted chicken pieces
Butter or margarine, melted

Pour rice into ungreased 9x13-inch dish. Pour soups over rice. Add water. Stir slightly to blend in soup and water. Dip chicken into butter and place skin side up in baking dish. Cover with foil and cook at 375° for 1 hour. Uncover and broil to brown chicken. **Serves 6 to 8.**

Serve chicken with Spinach and Strawberry Salad on page 129.

GRAM'S SOUP

Mrs. Paul Mnoian
Arcadia, CA

My very own old, old recipe I have used for my three sons, and now it is a favorite of all my grandchildren.

They say, *"I will just have Gram's Soup."*

2 cans (10½ ounces each) clear chicken broth
½ pound ground round, formed into patty
½ cup long grain rice, uncooked
1 medium carrot, sliced
¾ cup elbow macaroni, uncooked
¼ cup large noodles, uncooked

In a medium saucepan with cover, simmer chicken broth and ground meat patty for 5 minutes. Add the rice and the sliced carrots. Cover pan and simmer for 15 minutes. Add the elbow macaroni and noodles. Cover pan, and cook for 10 minutes more on low heat. **Serves 4 to 6.**

CHICKEN VELVET SOUP

Jane (Mrs. John K., Jr.)
Dunne
Dallas, TX

"There is nothing like this soup to cure your ills and make you feel warm and secure. Mommy always makes this when we are sick, facing exams or difficult times."

1½ sticks butter
¾ cup flour
1 cup milk
1 cup heavy cream
6 cups chicken broth
2 cups chicken, cooked and finely chopped
Salt and white pepper to taste
Fresh parsley, chopped

Make a roux with the butter and flour and cook for 2 minutes. In a separate saucepan, heat milk, heavy cream and broth and add a little at a time to roux until mixture thickens. Blend until smooth. When soup starts to boil, add chicken and seasonings; cook an additional 5 minutes. Garnish with chopped parsley. **Serves 8.**

Serve soup with bread sticks and butter.

GREEK LEMON SOUP

Cindy Kypreos
Fort Worth, TX

Old family recipe my mother used to serve us as children whenever anyone had a cold. The kids say, *"Is somebody sick?"*

3 cups chicken stock
½ cup rice or orzo, uncooked
2 eggs, beaten
3 tablespoons lemon juice, freshly squeezed
1 teaspoon lemon pepper
½ teaspoon salt

Boil chicken stock. Stir in rice. Lower heat to simmer and cook rice 20 minutes. Beat eggs in mixing bowl or blender. Add lemon juice and continue beating. Add the stock a little at a time to keep the eggs from curdling, mix well. Then pour back in soup pot on low heat until ready to serve. **Serves 4.**

Serve soup with salted crackers and cheese.

GOOD NEIGHBOR POTATO SOUP

Martha B. Hunt
Houston, TX

There is something about potatoes that soothes the soul. Tucked up in bed with a cold or flu, surrounded by stuffed animals and books, sick is still sick. A child needs food that tastes like love, and potato soup fills the bill.

2 cups celery, diced
1½ cups raw potatoes, diced
¼ cup onion, diced
2 cups chicken stock
1½ tablespoons cornstarch
2 cups milk
1½ teaspoons salt
¼ teaspoon white pepper
1 tablespoon butter
1 cup Cheddar cheese, grated

Simmer celery, potatoes and onion in stock, covered, for 15 minutes or until tender. Mix the cornstarch and milk, add to the vegetable mixture. Heat just to the boiling point and quickly remove from heat; do not boil. Add seasonings. Top with cheese. **Serves 6 to 8.**

Serve soup with Cheese Roll-Ups on page 40, and tea.

BOILED CUSTARD

Susan Brodarick
St. Louis, MO

In my family this recipe is considered a good remedy for whatever ails you. As children, we always alerted my mother or grandmother to any ache or pain, knowing that one of them would instantly make this recipe. We would immediately begin to feel better.

"Boiled Custard is the best medicine there is!"

7½ cups milk
6 egg yolks
8 heaping tablespoons sugar
3 tablespoons flour
⅛ teaspoon salt
2 teaspoons vanilla extract

Heat milk in a double boiler to just below boiling point. In mixing bowl, combine egg yolks, sugar, flour and salt. Add hot milk a little at a time to egg mixture, stirring constantly. Return to stove and cook, stirring constantly over low heat until mixture coats spoon or until slightly thickened. It will thicken more when chilled. When cool, add 2 teaspoons vanilla extract. Store in refrigerator. **Serves 6.**

The custard may be served in a parfait glass or poured over ice cream as a sauce. Or you can drink it like a milk shake.

CHILDREN'S "QUICK TEA"

Mrs. Beth A. Crowe
Greenwich, CT

While shopping at Neiman Marcus I found the most enchanting children's tea set . . . the design is of a cat dancing with a garland of flowers. I have two little boys and I was thrilled to find a unisex tea set. We have had many *"tea"* parties to date.

1 cup milk
1 tablespoon vanilla extract
1 lump sugar or 1 teaspoon honey

Combine ingredients and microwave 60 seconds. **Serves 1.**

Serve tea with cinnamon sticks and scones.

FRESH FRUIT SMOOTHIE

Angela Paulsen
Sunriver, OR

The one and only quote from Andreas is *"I want my smoovie, Mummie."*

5 medium strawberries, stemmed
⅓ cup plain yogurt
⅓ banana
½ cup orange juice
1 cup ice

Place all ingredients into a blender and process until ice is finely chopped. **Serves 1.**

Serve with blueberry bagels and cream cheese.

ORANGE SUNSHINE

Mrs. Happy Dumas
Hillsborough, CA

½ can (6 ounces) frozen orange juice
½ cup milk
½ cup water
¼ cup sugar
½ teaspoon vanilla extract
6 ice cubes

Mix all ingredients together in a blender. **Serves 2.**

Serve shake with cinnamon rolls and butter.

SUNNY SMILE

Mrs. Earl H. Schafer
Newport Beach, CA

This is very simple, but children love it and it is nourishing and tastes a lot like ORANGE JULIUS.® My children continue to make it themselves as they grow older.

1 can frozen orange juice
2 cans water
1 or 2 eggs, raw
1 teaspoon vanilla extract
1 teaspoon sugar

Combine ingredients in blender until well mixed. **Serves 4.**

Serve shake with granola bars.

COOKING TERMS

1. **Clarified Butter** - Butter is clarified by gentle heating. A white deposit forms on the bottom of the pan and the clear butter can be poured off.

2. **Egg Wash** - An egg white mixed with 1 tablespoon water and brushed on a bread, pie crust or cookie prior to baking to give the surface a glossy look.

3. **Hard-ball Stage** - Stage in candy making when the syrup, as it drops into cold water, forms a hard ball. (245°F to 250°F)

4. **Julienne** - A method of cutting vegetables and other food into thin strips about the length of a matchstick and ⅛-inch wide.

5. **Lemon Zest** - Shavings of the yellow part only of the rind of the lemon. The white part is bitter, and while some recipes call for this, when "lemon zest" is mentioned, use the yellow part only.

6. **Piping** - To make a decorative edge around a dessert using frosting that has been placed in a pastry bag with a decorating tip on the end. Squeeze the icing from the bag to form the design needed.

7. **Roux** - Equal quantities of butter and flour cooked together and used as a base for sauces or as a thickening agent.

8. **Tempering** - The process of warming eggs slowly by placing a small amount of hot mixture into eggs and stirring rapidly to keep the eggs from curdling. Once a portion of the eggs have been warmed, the eggs and mixture can be combined without curdling.

WEIGHTS & MEASURES

1 quart = 4 cups = 64 tablespoons = 32 fluid ounces
1 pint = 2 cups = 32 tablespoons = 16 fluid ounces
½ pint = 1 cup = 16 tablespoons = 8 fluid ounces
1 tablespoon = 3 teaspoons = ½ fluid ounce
Dash = less than ⅛ teaspoon

Metric liquid measurements:
3.785 liters = 1 gallon
.9463 liters = 1 quart
.4732 liters = 1 pint
¼ liter, approximately = 1 cup

Metric dry measurements:
1.101 liters = 1 quart
.551 liters = 1 pint

Metric Weights:
30 grams, approximately = 1 ounce
454 grams, approximately = 1 pound

All temperatures are given in degrees Fahrenheit (°F).
To convert °F to °C, subtract 32°, multiply by 5, and divide by 9.

INDEX

LISTING OF CONTRIBUTORS

CONTRIBUTORS

L—
Chris Larson—Fort Worth, TX, 110
Mrs. Alfred W. Lasher, Jr.—Houston, TX, 191
Zita Lefebure—Beverly Hills, CA, 140
Barbara G. Levin—Winnetka, IL, 172
Sarah Salter Levy—Weston, MA, 38
Joan Lunden—New York, NY, 109
Michèle d'Arlin Lynch—Los Angeles, CA, 211

M—
Lois Jean MacFarlane—Kiawah Island, SC, 109
Katherine B. Madden—Dayton, OH, 137
Sandra Mallin—Las Vegas, NV, 43
Debra Marcus—Laguna Niguel, CA, 21
Dr. Roberta H. Markman—Huntington Beach, CA, 194
Marian Marshall—New York, NY, 156
Mary Martens—Chesterfield, MO, 215
Sandra Matteucci—Phoenix, AZ, 101
Denise McCoy—Houston, TX, 242
Ann (Mrs. Craig) McDonald—Ralls, TX, 103
Margaret H. McFarland—Houston, TX, 228
Mary McGee—Norman, OK, 43
Chef Doug McNeill, Four Seasons Hotel
Washington, D.C., 158
Frances Mead-Messinger—Huntington Beach, CA, 150
Karen Merz—Atlanta, GA, 187
Ruth Reva Michaelson—Aurora, CO, 120
Susan M. Miller—Chesterfield, MO, 68
Ronnie and Joyce Milsap—Nashville, TN, 47
Mrs. Paul Mnoian—Arcadia, CA, 243
Mrs. Guy Edward Moman—Tuscaloosa, AL, 67
Elaine Montgomery—Garland, TX, 110
Pamela Morse—Houston, TX, 87
Anne Marie Morton—Houston, TX, 139

N—
Alene Nardick—Northbrook, IL, 213
Donivee Nash—Arcadia, CA, 119
Terry Naster—Naperville, IL, 48
Jim Nedohon—Arlington, VA, 206
Mrs. William J. Nesbitt—Shreveport, LA, 239
Mrs. Robin Nigro—White Plains, NY, 204
Constance B. Norris—Oak Ridge, TX, 29
Gloria Nycek—Dearborn, MI, 149

O—
Billy O'Connor, Jr.—Dallas, TX, 182
Lynn M. (Mrs. Donald S.) Osen—Laguna Beach, CA, 124
Mrs. Arthur L. Owen—Dallas, TX, 56

P—
Patsy J. (Mrs. Arnold) Palmer—Los Angeles, CA, 77
Susan Panish—Boston, MA, 167
Dorothea M. Park—Warren, PA, 107
Christine Elise Parrott—St. Louis, MO, 229
Angela Paulsen—Sunriver, OR, 247
Kay (Nina) Peeples—Houston, TX, 178
Gail Pettigrew—Richardson, TX, 40
Mrs. Ronald C. Prati, Sr.—Dallas, TX, 205
Mrs. Leslie (Laquita) Price, Jr.—Tyronza, AR, 128
Leslie Marie Price—Pasadena, TX, 22
Shirley Pruitt—Corona del Mar, CA, 125
Wolfgang Puck—Beverly Hills, CA, 36

R—
Mickie Rabinowitz—Plantation, FL, 220
Teresa D. Rajala, M.D.—Allen, TX, 85
Evy Rappaport—Beverly Hills, CA, 225
Mrs. Adinah W. Raskas—St. Louis, MO, 222
Sherrie Reddick—Wichita Falls, TX, 190
Ruth Ann Renick—Rolla, MO, 104
Governor Ann W. Richards—Austin, TX, 226
Stan Richards—Dallas, TX, 147
Marcialea Rittenberg—Marina del Rey, CA, 155
Roxanne Rivera—Tijeras, NM, 95
Susan Roberds—Dallas, TX, 195
Mrs. Leonard Rosenberg—Houston, TX, 221
Vicki Rosholt—Minneapolis, MN, 218
Mrs. Ruth Ruder—Cincinnati, OH, 164

S—
Betty Ann Samson—Atlanta, GA, 38
Mr. & Mrs. V. W. Sanders—Port Hueneme, CA, 31
Elizabeth Scarff—Jackson, MS, 143
Mrs. Earl H. Schafer—Newport Beach, CA, 247
Mrs. C. W. Schoenvogel—College Station, TX, 105
Mrs. S. C. (Sam) Schultz—Marietta, GA, 212
Sharon Schwartz—Houston, TX, 62
Courtney H. Scott—Spartanburg, SC, 180
Elizabeth E. Solender & Gary L. Scott—Dallas, TX, 75
Kathy Scott—Atlanta, GA, 183
Betty Lynn Seidmon, Ph.D.—Daytona Beach, FL, 83
Betty (Mrs. William) Seitz—Dallas, TX, 152
Amy Severs—Rowlett, TX, 168
Amanda Shams—Atlanta, GA, 50
Saundra Reiter Shapiro—Marietta, GA, 90
Karen Sheetz—Newport Beach, CA, 78
Joan L. Sheppard—Godfrey, IL, 26
Ellen Sherwood—Chesterfield, MO, 165
Joyce Shlesinger—Atlanta, GA, 214
Gail Silverman—Dallas, TX, 23
Tamara (Tami) Silvestri—Dallas, TX, 32
Nancy Skuble—Santa Monica, CA, 145
Nancy (Mrs. Kent) Snyder—Laguna Beach, CA, 233
Melissa A. Spatz—Atlanta, GA, 160
Mara Squar—Tarzana, CA, 130
Heather Stern—Chicago, IL, 106
Janet Stevenson—Kansas City, MO, 88
Mrs. Joan A. Stewart—Houston, TX, 153
Mrs. Anne E. Sullivan—Newburyport, MA, 232
Laurel Sung—Dallas, TX, 89
Linda Svehlak—Dallas, TX, 182
Eileen H. Swartz—Swampscott, MA, 223
Bonnie B. Swearingen—Chicago, IL, 166
Janet Swedburg—Axtell, NE, 127

T—
Mrs. Ileen Tabankin—Naperville, IL, 98
Kim L. Temple—Dallas, TX, 45
Mrs. K. R. Tharp—Dallas, TX, 238
Deborah (Debbie) Thomas—Dallas, TX, 170
Marlo Thomas—New York, NY, 151
Nancy (Mrs. Donald C.) Thomas—Indian Wells, CA, 188
Terre Thomas—Beverly Hills, CA, 86
Mrs. Joe S. Thompson—Sherman, TX, 172
Richard Ford Thompson—Dallas, TX, 216
Mrs. Tignor M. Thompson—Dallas, TX, 84
Teresa Thrash—Tyler, TX, 26
Clarice Tinsley-Giles—Dallas, TX, 162
Susan Mullins Tipler—Birmingham, AL, 202
Linda Tondu—Houston, TX, 138

V—
Lynne Valentine—Balboa Island, CA, 128
Taryn M. Valle—Newton Center, MA, 168

W—
Marianne Waid—Atlanta, GA, 238
Catherine Walker—Los Gatos, CA, 108
Kae Walters—Cincinnati, OH, 101
Ruth Wander—Highland Park, IL, 217
Mrs. Marjorie H. Watkins—Glencoe, IL, 37
Mr. & Mrs. Ben R. Weber, Jr.—Dallas, TX, 131
Delores (Mrs. Thomas) Wehling—St. Charles, IL, 209
Evelyn W. Weissman—Lawrence, NY, 146
Laura Wertheimer—Washington, DC, 189
Brady White—Los Angeles, CA, 234
Sharon L. Whitley—Frisco, TX, 200
Judith H. Willers—Agoura Hills, CA, 52
Betty (Mrs. Eddie) Williams—Arlington, TX, 186
Willie B. Wilson—Dallas, TX, 41
Jean S. Wong—San Francisco, CA, 54
Nancy Wright—Marietta, GA, 243

Y—
Mitchell Yoffe—Stamford, CT, 142

Z—
Sue Zelickson—Minneapolis, MN, 173

PLEASE CUT ALONG DOTTED LINES

I would like to order additional copies of Neiman Marcus Cookbooks:

☐ *Pigtails and Froglegs* ____ quantity ☐ *Pure & Simple* ____ quantity

☐ FOR MYSELF ☐ AS A GIFT ☐ FOR MYSELF ☐ AS A GIFT

MAIL TO: NAME ______________________________

ADDRESS ______________________________

CITY, STATE, ZIP ______________________________

IF GIFT, GIFT CARD SHOULD READ: ______________________________

____

ENCLOSED IS MY CHECK OR PLEASE CHARGE MY ACCOUNT, $19.95 PLUS $3.95 SHIPPING PLUS ANY APPLICABLE TAXES: ☐ NEIMAN MARCUS ☐ AMERICAN EXPRESS

ACCOUNT # ______________________________ EXP. DATE ______________

SIGNATURE ______________________________

Mail to: Neiman Marcus Cookbooks • P.O. Box 3188 • Dallas, TX 75221
or call: 1-800-624-7253

PLEASE CUT ALONG DOTTED LINES

I would like to order additional copies of Neiman Marcus Cookbooks:

☐ *Pigtails and Froglegs* ____ quantity ☐ *Pure & Simple* ____ quantity

☐ FOR MYSELF ☐ AS A GIFT ☐ FOR MYSELF ☐ AS A GIFT

MAIL TO: NAME ______________________________

ADDRESS ______________________________

CITY, STATE, ZIP ______________________________

IF GIFT, GIFT CARD SHOULD READ: ______________________________

____

ENCLOSED IS MY CHECK OR PLEASE CHARGE MY ACCOUNT, $19.95 PLUS $3.95 SHIPPING PLUS ANY APPLICABLE TAXES: ☐ NEIMAN MARCUS ☐ AMERICAN EXPRESS

ACCOUNT # ______________________________ EXP. DATE ______________

SIGNATURE ______________________________

Mail to: Neiman Marcus Cookbooks • P.O. Box 3188 • Dallas, TX 75221
or call: 1-800-624-7253

PLEASE CUT ALONG DOTTED LINES

I would like to order additional copies of Neiman Marcus Cookbooks:

☐ *Pigtails and Froglegs* ____ quantity ☐ *Pure & Simple* ____ quantity

☐ FOR MYSELF ☐ AS A GIFT ☐ FOR MYSELF ☐ AS A GIFT

MAIL TO: NAME ______________________________

ADDRESS ______________________________

CITY, STATE, ZIP ______________________________

IF GIFT, GIFT CARD SHOULD READ: ______________________________

____

ENCLOSED IS MY CHECK OR PLEASE CHARGE MY ACCOUNT, $19.95 PLUS $3.95 SHIPPING PLUS ANY APPLICABLE TAXES: ☐ NEIMAN MARCUS ☐ AMERICAN EXPRESS

ACCOUNT # ______________________________ EXP. DATE ______________

SIGNATURE ______________________________

Mail to: Neiman Marcus Cookbooks • P.O. Box 3188 • Dallas, TX 75221
or call: 1-800-624-7253

CARROT SEED